# GOD,
## Help Me Experience More of You

### KAY ARTHUR

HARVEST HOUSE PUBLISHERS

EUGENE, OREGON

Verses marked NASB are taken from the New American Standard Bible®, © 1960, 1962, 1963, 1968, 1971, 1972, 1973, 1975, 1977, 1995 by The Lockman Foundation. Used by permission. (www.Lockman.org)

References marked KJV are taken from the King James Version of the Bible.

*Cover by Koechel Peterson & Associates, Inc., Minneapolis, Minnesota*

## GOD, HELP ME EXPERIENCE MORE OF YOU

Text taken from *My Savior, My Friend*
Copyright © 1995 by Kay Arthur
Published by Harvest House Publishers

Library of Congress Cataloging-in-Publication Data

Arthur, Kay, 1933-
    God, help me to experience more of you / Kay Arthur.
      p. cm.
    Portion of text from My Savior, my friend.
    Includes bibliographical references.
    ISBN 0-7369-1069-7 (pbk.)
    1. Bible. N.T. John I-IX—Meditations. I. Title.
BS2615.54.A78 2003
226.5'06—dc22                                                                        2003017855

**Printed in the United States of America.**

04  05  06  07  /  VP-MS  /  10  9  8  7  6  5  4  3  2  1

# Contents

# Jesus Reveals God the Father in All His Glory

## JOHN 1–4

*1*

*D*ear Reader,

Among the Gospels, John holds a unique place. The Synoptic Gospels—Matthew, Mark, and Luke—focus on the humanity of Jesus Christ and were written basically within the same time period of A.D. 55 to 68. The Gospel of John, however, was not written until between A.D. 85 and 90. John was written to prove without a shadow of doubt that Jesus was truly and fully God while being truly and fully man.

In Matthew, written between A.D. 58 and 68, we behold Jesus the King. In Mark, written between A.D. 55 and 65, we behold Jesus the servant. In Luke, written between A.D. 60 and 68, we see Jesus as the perfect man, with emphasis on the virgin birth of our Lord and, of course, on a detailed genealogy that takes us all the way back to Adam.

In John, we behold Jesus as God, one with the Father, the One whose name is I AM. And since God has no genealogy, John simply takes us back to the beginning when "the Word was with God, and the Word was God" (John 1:1). And in his majestic introduction, John sweeps us from the beginning to the fullness of time when "the Word became flesh, and dwelt among us, and we saw His glory, glory as of the only begotten from the Father, full of grace and truth" (John 1:14). In John, we see Jesus, the divine Son, "the only begotten God who is in the bosom of the Father" (John 1:18) and who comes to earth to explain the Father.

O Beloved, as we devotionally examine part of this divine Gospel, may the eyes of your heart eagerly drink in the beauty of the relationship of the Son to His Father. Keep your eyes on Jesus, the One who will explain to you the Father heart of God, who loved you so much "that He gave His only begotten Son" so that you would not perish but have everlasting life (John 3:16).

Before we start, let me give you an overview of the entire book of John. Then, as we move into the study of the first 11 chapters of John's Gospel, I pray that you will know an insatiable longing to abide in Him and to have His words abide in you.

## Experiencing God in the Person of Jesus

JOHN 1—You will see Jesus proclaimed as "the Lamb of God" who will take away your sins (1:36).

JOHN 2—You will hear Him say that He is the temple of God, destroyed by men, but raised by the Father (2:19).

JOHN 3—Jesus shows us how He is like the serpent in the wilderness—raised up so that those who look to Him shall not die though bitten by the serpent (3:14).

JOHN 4—He is the Christ who satisfies your deepest needs so that you never thirst again (4:14).

JOHN 5—We see Him as the Son of God, doing nothing on His own initiative but always and only doing those things which please the Father (5:30).

JOHN 6—We see that Jesus is the True Bread that has come down from God out of heaven so that we might eat and live forever (6:35).

JOHN 7—Jesus cries that those who thirst should come to Him, for He is the Fountain of Living Water. He assures us that those who believe in Him shall have rivers of living water flowing from their innermost beings (7:37,38).

JOHN 8—Having forgiven the woman taken in adultery, He turns to those walking in darkness and proclaims that those who follow Him shall not walk in the darkness but shall have the light of life, because He is the Light of Life (8:12). And so you cannot miss it, in this chapter Jesus explains that if you do not believe that He is God, the I AM, you shall die in your sins (8:24).

JOHN 9—Jesus is seen as the Son of Man who gives sight to the blind (9:39).

JOHN 10—We hear the voice of the Good Shepherd calling His sheep by name, and then laying down His life for them so they will never perish but will have eternal life (10:3,11).

**JOHN 11**—We hear Him promise Martha that He is the resurrection and the life, and that anyone who believes in Him shall live even if he dies (11:25).

**JOHN 12**—His hour has finally come. It is time for the Son of Man to be glorified, for the grain of wheat to fall into the ground and die so that it can bear much fruit (12:23,24).

**JOHN 13**—We find our Teacher and Lord girding Himself with a towel and washing His disciples' feet—leaving us an example of love's servanthood (13:14-17).

**JOHN 14**—We hear Jesus, the express image of the Father, telling us that through the gift of the Holy Spirit we shall do the works that He did because He is going to the Father (14:12).

**JOHN 15**—We see how life in Him is possible. We discover that He is the Vine and that we are the branches, and we come to understand that through abiding in Him, we bear much fruit (15:5).

**JOHN 16**—Jesus explains that He must go away so that He can send the Holy Spirit as our Helper who shall guide us into all truth (16:7,13).

**JOHN 17**—Our hearts burn as we hear our High Priest interceding on our behalf with the Father, asking that we might be one even as They are one (17:22).

**JOHN 18**—Jesus stands before Pilate as the King of the Jews, and the crowd shouts, "Not this Man, but Barabbas" (18:37,40).

**JOHN 19**—We look upon the Crucified One, the Son who cries, "*Tetélestai*—It is finished!" (19:30).

**JOHN 20**—Death is conquered! The tomb is empty! Jesus becomes the Giver of Life (20:21-23).

**JOHN 21**—As Lord He says, "Tend My lambs....Shepherd My sheep....Follow Me!" (21:15,16,19).

## 2

*F*rom the very beginning, John makes his purpose clear: to establish that Jesus is God. This fact is critical and essential. To miss His deity is to miss salvation! Thus, John takes us back to the beginning when there was no one but the Father, the Spirit, and the Logos, the Word: "In the beginning was the Word, and the Word was with God, and the Word was God. He was in the beginning with God. All things came into being through Him, and apart from Him nothing came into being that has come into being. In Him was life, and the life was the Light of men" (John 1:1-4).

John wants to make sure we know that life is found only in one place—in God's Son. At a later date, John will write another epistle in which he says, "He that hath the Son hath life; and he that hath not the Son of God hath not life" (1 John 5:12 KJV). It is that simple, Beloved. Apart from Jesus, you are dead in your trespasses and sins. You are among the living dead who will never pass from death to life unless they receive Jesus Christ for who He is—God and the only Savior of the world.

"But as many as received Him, to them He gave the right to become children of God, even to those who believe in His name" (John 1:12). And how would God make it possible for sinful men, women, and children to become children of God?

The Word, the Logos, would become flesh and dwell among us so that we could behold His glory, "glory as of the only begotten from the Father, full of grace and truth" (John 1:14). Jesus, "the only begotten God who is in the bosom of the Father" (John 1:18), would explain the Father to us. Then through His death, burial, and resurrection, Jesus would become "the way, and the truth, and the life" (John 14:6) by whom we might come to the Father. And grace and truth would be realized through Jesus Christ (John 1:17).

O Beloved, have you ever really laid hold of the truth of all that Jesus is: the eternal Logos, the Creator of the world, the Son of God, the Light of life, God in the flesh? Has His grace—His pleasure, His delight, His favorable regard, His graciousness, His lovingkindness, His goodwill, His unmerited favor—ever overwhelmed you so as to save you from death and hell and give you life, eternal and abundant?

The Law given through Moses condemns; grace pardons. The Law exposes our sin; grace covers it. The Law diagnoses our illness; grace cures it. The Law shuts us up and plays the demanding schoolmaster; grace provides us with an indwelling Teacher, the Holy Spirit, and liberates us! "For the Law was given through Moses; grace and truth were realized through Jesus Christ" (John 1:17).

Read John 1:1-18 and think upon these things.

*3*

*D*o you have a hard time relating to God the Father? Maybe it is because your earthly father fell so drastically short of what a father should be! Maybe your father divorced your mother and left you father-less. Maybe you could never please your father and always fell short of his expectations. Perhaps your father was too busy to spend time with you. He merely gave orders and dished out punishment when you didn't do what you were supposed to. Maybe you were molested, abused, or beaten by your father. You picture God as someone to fear because you wonder if He, too, will wrong you if you ever give Him an opportunity.

O Beloved, I understand how hard it may be to entrust yourself to another Father when your experience has been horrendous or void of anything meaningful. And yet, there is a bridge that will span all of that! The Lord Jesus Christ is the bridge which enables you to experience the fullness of all that a child should know and have in a father.

John tells us that it is Jesus who explains to us the Father (1:18). Jesus says, "He who sees Me sees the One who sent Me" (12:45). "If you had known Me, you would have known My Father also" (14:7). "He who has seen Me has seen the Father" (14:9). He could say this because He was one with the Father (10:30); the Father was abiding in Him (14:10).

Jesus came that you might have God for your Father—a perfect Father who loves you unconditionally, a Father who will never leave you nor forsake you. A Father who will always come to your aid, a Father who loves you so much that He gave up His only begotten Son that you might have life and have it abundantly!

Just before Jesus died, He prayed to the Father on our behalf: "Holy Father, keep them in Your name, the name which You have given Me, that they may be one even as We are" (John 17:11). Oneness with the Father—eternal oneness—enveloped in His love forever and ever. It is this relationship that God wants you to understand and embrace. He sent His Son to explain Himself to you! He longs to be your Father God.

O Beloved, why don't you read through the Gospel of John beginning with chapter 1 and reading a chapter each day. As you read, list in a notebook all that you learn about Jesus Christ as He explains the Father. Keep this notebook with your Bible and this book, so that as you spend time with the Father in the Gospel of John you can write down what He is teaching you. I'll ask you to make some notes on things we do together. It will be exciting to look back later at all you learned! In the meantime, day by day, as you weave each truth into a blanket of security, you can snuggle warm and secure in its truth. It will set you free from misconceptions of the fatherhood of God, which would keep you from trusting Him.

# 4

$\mathcal{W}$ouldn't it be wonderful to know and understand why God created you? Don't you long to realize His purpose for your life and to live within the context of that purpose? John the Baptist knew and lived accordingly. "There came a man sent from God, whose name was John. He came as a witness, to testify about the Light, so that all might believe through him. He was not the Light, but he came to testify about the Light" (John 1:6-8).

*Testify* or *witness* is a key word in the Gospel of John. How well it fits with John's purpose! The Greek word[1] for *witness* or *testify* is *martus* or *martur:* "one who can or does affirm what he knows, has seen, or heard." From this word we get our English word *martyr:* "one who bears witness by his death." How well this word describes John the Baptist, who was beheaded by Herod because he stood without compromise for righteousness.

Imagine what it was like when John the Baptist appeared in the wilderness, breaking God's 400 years of silence with the words, "Behold, the Lamb of God who takes away the sin of the world! This is He on behalf of whom I said, 'After me comes a Man who has a higher rank than I, for He existed before me'" (John 1:29,30).

Finally, the fullness of time had come, bringing the long- awaited Messiah. Once John the Baptist bore witness, others, upon seeing Jesus, knew that John's witness was true. Andrew introduced his brother Simon Peter to Jesus saying, "'We have found the Messiah' (which translated means Christ)" (John 1:41). And when Philip met Jesus, he found Nathanael and said to him, "We have found Him of whom Moses in the Law and also the Prophets wrote—Jesus of Nazareth, the son of Joseph" (John 1:45). When Nathanael met Jesus, he said, "Rabbi, You are the Son of God; You are the King of Israel" (John 1:49). What was happening? As each one met and recognized Jesus, they bore witness to others of Christ!

O Beloved, I can tell you one sure purpose for your life, and that is to bear witness of what you know about your Lord and your God. Are you affirming to others what you have seen and known about Jesus Christ? That's a witness! Don't be afraid of it—just tell others what you know. God will do the rest!

# 5

Is God concerned about the little things in your life that seemingly have nothing to do with the spiritual realm? Yes, He is! I pray for parking places! When I can't find something, I keep asking, "Father, show me where it is." Whether I find the item or not doesn't affect a single soul's salvation, nor does it affect the course of the church. Yet, I constantly talk to my Father about the everyday things of life.

Some people might say, "God is too busy running the universe to be troubled with parking places and lost articles!" But is He? Let's look together at John 2 and see what we can find in that chapter that might give us some insight.

Here we have an account of the first sign ever performed by our Lord. The very recording of this event gives it great significance. On the surface, it does not seem to be an earthshaking miracle, especially if you compare it to miracles which result in the lame walking, the blind seeing, and the dead rising. In John 2, Jesus turns water into wine. Now granted, it was an enormous amount of wine (120 to 180 gallons), and it was the best wine they had ever tasted—far better than the host had served!

This sign clearly demonstrated Jesus' power over the elements. Yet there is another significant reason for this miracle. Jesus turned water into wine to save a family embarrassment and shame. In those days, weddings were very important events. A host was obligated to have ample wine. After all, hadn't he drunk amply at the weddings of his friends? To run out of wine would not only embarrass him greatly, but would put him in their debt. Jesus changed water into wine because He cared about the plight of His host.

Jesus cares! He cares about everything that has to do with you! And because He cares, you know that your Father God cares. Remember, Jesus is explaining the Father to you. That is why He tells us in 1 Peter 5:7 to cast "all your anxiety on Him, because He cares for you."

Jesus didn't turn water into wine to astound a crowd or simply to prove His power over the elements. He had just told His mother, "My hour has not yet come" (John 2:4), so we know that He did not perform the miracle to demonstrate His deity. No, Jesus performed this sign because of a need, to save the host from great embarrassment.

Tuck that thought into your heart today. Treasure it. Your Father God cares about your daily everythings that concern you. Run to Him with everything. He loves it!

# 6

*T*wice in His ministry Jesus cleansed the Temple, throwing out the moneychangers. His first encounter with these men was at the beginning of His public ministry. The second was at the end. In fact, the final cleansing was the crushing blow that brought Him to the house of Annas, then to Caiaphas, both of whom profited from the sales in the Temple area. Zeal for His Father's house consumed our Lord. They were making His "Father's house a place of business" (John 2:16).

I wonder what would happen if Jesus visited many of the ministries around the world today. What would He find? What would He do? He always sees beyond the apparent, beyond what we say to the very heart attitude that motivates us. Christian leaders need to walk in great integrity!

The first cleansing of the Temple in Jerusalem caused the Jews to ask, "'What sign do You show us as your authority for doing these things?' Jesus answered them, 'Destroy this temple, and in three days I will raise it up.' The Jews then said, 'It took forty-six years to build this temple, and will You raise it up in three days?' But He was speaking of the temple of His body. So when He was raised from the dead, His disciples remembered that He said this" (John 2:18-22).

The resurrection of Jesus Christ from the dead would be the ultimate of signs! Yet it is this sign that most people stumble over, coming up with all sorts of lame explanations to rationalize what happened to the body of Jesus Christ during and after His crucifixion.

Some say that Jesus never died on the cross: "He merely swooned, and the coolness of the tomb revived Him." But to that we would have to ask, "What about the blood and water that poured forth from His side when the soldier thrust in his spear?" (John 19:34). Blood and water are a sign of a ruptured heart.

Others say that His body was stolen. If so, the disciples pulled off quite a feat with that many soldiers guarding the tomb! If the disciples took the body, were they foolish enough to die martyrs' deaths for Someone who did not rise from the dead?

Others say, "But where are the witnesses of His resurrection, other than the deluded apostles?" Is 500 enough —"at one time," no less? First Corinthians 15:6 tells us of this sighting by 500 to which the skeptics say, "But that is in the Bible!" As a book of historical evidence and authenticity, there is more manuscript evidence of the Bible—both Old and New Testaments—than there is for other works we accept as genuine.

O Beloved, when you deal with skeptics and the Word of God, never forget you're in spiritual warfare against the god of this world who has blinded their eyes—even of religious people! It was the same in Jesus' day.

# 7

The Jews asked for a sign, and Jesus gave them sign after sign. Even after the ultimate of signs, His resurrection, they still refused to believe. Beginning in chapter 2 of his Gospel, the apostle John records for us a select number of signs which will prove beyond a shadow of a doubt that Jesus is the Christ, the Messiah, the Promised One foretold by the prophets. Then John writes, "Many other signs Jesus also performed in the presence of the disciples, which are not written in this book; but these have been written so that you may believe..." (John 20:30,31).

Three different Greek words are used to describe the supernatural works which Jesus performed during His public ministry. John, however, uses only one of these: *sign(s)*. The Greek word for *sign(s)* is *smeion,* and is used in John 2:11,18, 23; 3:2; 4:48,54; 6:2,14,26,30; 7:31; 9:16; 10:41; 11:47; 12:18,37; and 20:30. Except for the resurrection, which is referred to as a sign in John 2:18,19, all the signs are recorded in the first segment of his Gospel. It is interesting that John preferred to use *smeion* over the other two Greek words translated "miracles"—*dunamis,* a supernatural power; and "wonders"—*teras,* something strange that causes awe.

Yet *smeion* is John's choice—the Holy Spirit's, really. This word carries with it a sense of going beyond the miracle, the wonder, the awe of it all, to note the significance of the sign itself. A sign (*smeion)* was an indication, an attesting. Signs appeal to the understanding, while wonders appeal to the eyes and imagination. Through the signs, John wants us to believe that Jesus is the Christ, not just another good man. As we will see in John 3, Jesus' signs did capture attention and attest to His deity! Nicodemus came to Jesus at night and said, "Rabbi, we know that You have come from God as a teacher; for no one can do these signs that You do unless God is with him" (John 3:2).

John records signs which show that Jesus is Lord, Master over all. He records five signs that no other Gospel mentions: water into wine, healing the royal official's son, the man lame for 38 years, the blind man, and raising of Lazarus from the dead.

Take some time now, Beloved, to look up each use of the word *sign(s)* in the Gospel of John. Remember, I gave these to you earlier as we began today. In your notebook, list each sign and note what Jesus is Master over. I know that you will be blessed and encouraged, for your Lord is still Master over all and that includes you!

*8*

$\mathcal{W}$hy must we be born again in order to enter the kingdom of God? Why can't God accept us the way we are? Why is a new birth necessary? And how does one go about being born again?

We want to answer these valid questions as we move on to John 3. So, before you go further, stop and read this chapter. The Word of God is alive and powerful. It discerns the thoughts and intentions of your heart. It sets you free from that which isn't truth. There is a supernatural, life-giving power to the Word of God. Jesus says, "The words that I have spoken to you are spirit and are life" (John 6:63). Never, never, never neglect the Word of God, my dear friend.

We must be born again, or born from above, because we are born into sin and our hearts are deceitful and desperately wicked. We are spiritually dead and doomed to an eternal death unless we are born again.

Romans 5:12 explains our state: "Therefore, just as through one man sin entered into the world, and death through sin, and so death spread to all men, because all sinned." Jeremiah 17:9 says, "The heart is deceitful above all things, and desperately wicked: who can know it?" (KJV).

Is it any wonder then that we read in 1 Corinthians 15:50: "Flesh and blood cannot inherit the kingdom of God..."? We cannot enter the kingdom of God in our natural state. Something supernatural must change us. That supernatural event is the second birth! We must be born again.[2]

How is it possible to be born again? That's the question Nicodemus, a ruler of the Jews, had. He questioned Jesus: "How can a man be born when he is old? He cannot enter a second time into his mother's womb and be born, can he?" (John 3:4).

No! That is not the way a second birth is accomplished. Thus, Jesus answers, "Truly, truly, I say to you, unless one is born of water and the Spirit he cannot enter into the kingdom of God. That which is born of the flesh is flesh, and that which is born of the Spirit is spirit" (John 3:5,6).

Think on it, Beloved. Talk to your Father about it. I love you and appreciate your willingness to spend time in the Word of God so that you can know truth…and so that you can walk in a new level of intimacy with your Savior. May He become your dearest Friend, too!

# *9*

*H*ow can we be born again? If we have deceitful and desperately wicked hearts, how can we ever hope to enter the kingdom of heaven?

Let's listen again to Jesus' answer to Nicodemus: "Do not be amazed that I said to you, 'You must be born again.' The wind blows where it wishes and you hear the sound of it, but do not know where it comes from and where it is going; so is everyone who is born of the Spirit" (John 3:7,8).

Being born again is a supernatural happening like the wind. You don't see the wind; you only see its effects. You see the tree sway or the paper flutter.

What does Jesus mean when He says you must be "born of water and the Spirit" (John 3:5)? The Spirit of God brings us into the family of God by convicting us of sin, righteousness, and judgment (John 16:8). Then by His indwelling, He makes us new creatures in Christ Jesus, becoming our Helper, Guide, Instructor, and the Guarantee of our redemption (2 Corinthians 5:17; John 14:16,17,26; 16:13; Ephesians 1:13,14). Romans 8:9 spells it out clearly: "If anyone does not have the Spirit of Christ, he does not belong to Him."

But what does Jesus mean when He says we must be "born of water" (John 3:5)? This is a question scholars have debated over the years. Let me briefly share several interpretations so that you will be aware of differences of opinion. Then I will share my interpretation and why I hold to that position. You can then take the interpretations to the

Scriptures and to the Holy Spirit as your Teacher. The correct interpretation must agree with the whole teaching of God's Word.

Let's wait until tomorrow to look at these views. Today, thank the heavenly Father that He Himself has made a way for you to be born again.

# 10

*T*oday we will consider what it means to be born of water. As we look at the different opinions, I will number each for you so you can follow me easily.

1. Some believe that *water* refers to literal water and, therefore, is a reference to water baptism. They believe the reference signifies the water of repentance, which is connected with baptism. This view doesn't allow for salvation apart from water baptism. Some would use Titus 3:5,6 to support this belief: "He saved us, not on the basis of deeds which we have done in righteousness, but according to His mercy, by the washing of regeneration and renewing by the Holy Spirit, whom He poured out upon us richly through Jesus Christ our Savior."

2. A second view is that *water* symbolizes the cleansing work of the Holy Spirit; thus, the water refers to the Holy Spirit Himself. Proponents of this view translate John 3:5 in this way: "born of water, even the Spirit." Those who hold this view also use John 4:14 and 7:37,38 to support their belief that the Holy Spirit is synonymous with water. In both of these passages, the Holy Spirit is likened to "water springing up to eternal life" and to "rivers of living water."

3. Others believe that the use of *water* in this context is a reference to our physical birth. They stand on the fact that in order to be

born spiritually, we must first be born physically. This third interpretation of John 3:5 holds to the view that the reference to water refers
to the sack of water which is broken in the process of our physical birth.
Therefore, the reference to water is nothing more than this! Those who
hold this belief propose that John 3:5 is a parallel to the statement which
follows: "That which is born of the flesh is flesh, and that which is born
of the Spirit is spirit" (3:6).

4. The fourth view of John 3:5 is that *water* is a reference to the
Word of God. This is the view I hold, which, of course, does not automatically make it the correct view. However, I would like to explain
why I hold this particular interpretation. Whether you agree or not,
Beloved, as I explain my interpretation, you will learn a vital truth that
will help you to share the gospel with others, and also to interpret difficult passages.

Whenever you come to a passage that is hard to interpret, you
need to remember three things: 1) You must consider the whole
counsel of God. Scripture will not contradict Scripture. 2) You must
go from the known to the unknown. There are certain truths that
are obvious. Begin with what you know to be true because it is
clearly taught in the Word. 3) You should go from the clear to the
obscure. Don't strain at gnats and swallow camels. Don't get caught
up in the controversy of interpretation and miss what God wants
to say. Remember, the Scriptures were written for common people.
God chose the foolish so that "no man may boast before God";
"Christ Jesus...became to us wisdom from God" (1 Corinthians
1:27-30). Also, as helpful as a knowledge of Greek and Hebrew can
be, I still believe that a thorough knowledge of the whole counsel
of God is the best means of interpreting the Word of God. Scripture
interprets Scripture, and it never contradicts itself.

In John 3, there is much about salvation that is obvious, much that is sufficient to bring a man to salvation, whether or not he has the correct interpretation of "born of water." Why bother then with the meaning of this part of the passage? Because God tells us to study to show ourselves approved unto Him, workmen that need not be ashamed, "accurately handling the word of truth" (2 Timothy 2:15).

Tomorrow we are going to look at what the whole counsel of God teaches regarding being born again and why Jesus uses the term "born of water." However, today you need to simply remember what you learned about handling the Word of God.

## 11

What do we learn from the whole counsel of God regarding being born again? And why do I believe that "born of water" is a reference to the Word of God? Let me explain what the Bible teaches about being born into God's family, and I think you will see why I believe that "the water" in John 3:5 is synonymous with the Word. If we go back to John 1:12,13, we see that being born again is supernatural—not of man. John 1:12,13 says, "But as many as received Him, to them He gave the right to become children of God, even to those who believe in His name, who were born, not of blood nor of the will of the flesh nor of the will of man, but of God."

When any person is born again, it is because God is the instigator of salvation. The new birth doesn't occur because man wills it so. Nor is it a result of man's bloodline or because his flesh desired it. Man is born again by the will of God.

Let's look at some of the Greek words used in John 1:12,13. The word for *children* is *teknon,* denoting prominence in relation to birth. The Greek word for *son (huios)* refers more to our adoption as sons, to our heirship.

In John 1:12, the word *received* seems to be synonymous with "believe in His name." The verb *believe* is a present participle which indicates a present and continuous activity of faith. In other words, once you genuinely believe, you will keep on believing. The preposition *in* of "in His name" (1:12) is *eis* in the Greek and indicates more than acceptance of a statement. It implies resting in, trusting in, availing oneself of all that Jesus is.

Receiving and believing in Jesus, then, is not merely acknowledging the facts regarding who He is and what He has accomplished. It is rather accepting and trusting Him as Savior, the Lord God who is the only means of obtaining forgiveness of sins and life eternal.

The word for *born* in John 1:13 is *genna,* which means "to beget children." This begetting is of God, who is the Author of salvation.

Now that we have seen who initiates our birth, let me show you why I believe that *water* in John 3:5 is a reference to the Word of God. We'll look at the whole counsel of God by doing some cross-referencing.

In John 5:24, Jesus says, "Truly, truly, I say to you, he who hears My word, and believes Him who sent Me, has eternal life, and does not come into judgment, but has passed out of death into life." According to this passage, belief is preceded by hearing God's Word.

In James 1:18, we read, "In the exercise of His will He brought us forth by the word of truth." Watch the terminology used by God. "Brought us forth" is *apokue,* which means "to give birth to." It comes from *kue,* which means "to be pregnant." According to James, what does God use in order to effect our spiritual birth? The Word of God! Think about it, dear friend.

## 12

*I*f it is the Word of God that God uses to cause a person to be born again, truly it is a supernatural Word! "You have been born again not of seed *[spora]* which is perishable but imperishable, that is, through the living and enduring word of God. For, 'ALL FLESH IS LIKE GRASS, AND ALL ITS GLORY LIKE THE FLOWER OF GRASS. THE GRASS WITHERS, AND THE FLOWER FALLS OFF, BUT THE WORD OF THE LORD ENDURES FOREVER'" (1 Peter 1:23-25).

God is telling His children that it takes the Word of God for a person to be born again. Like the parable of the sower, the seed sown in our hearts is the Word of God (Mark 4:14). If we receive God's Word, believe it, put our trust and confidence in it, it results in our being born again. Why? Because it is an imperishable seed that endures forever and brings a man to belief. "'WHOEVER WILL CALL ON THE NAME OF THE LORD WILL BE SAVED.' How then will they call on Him in whom they have not believed? How will they believe in Him whom they have not heard? And how will they hear without a preacher? How will they preach unless they are sent? Just as it is written, 'HOW BEAUTIFUL ARE THE FEET OF THOSE WHO BRING GOOD NEWS OF GOOD THINGS!' However, they did not all heed the good news; for Isaiah says, 'LORD, WHO HAS BELIEVED OUR REPORT?' So faith comes from hearing, and hearing by the word of Christ" (Romans 10:13-17).

As you can see from this passage, calling upon the Lord brings salvation, but a person cannot call on Someone they do not know anything about! That is why God calls you and me to go forth as His witnesses, testifying to that which we have heard, seen, and learned about Jesus Christ and about the whole counsel of God's Word.

You don't need to be anxious about bringing about a decision for Jesus Christ—that is not your responsibility. As you have seen, salvation does not come by the will of man, by human power or persuasiveness. It comes by the will of God! Therefore, you simply sow the imperishable seed of God's Word and God gives the increase. Doesn't that take the pressure off? You are not responsible for another's salvation.

Elizabeth Neubold, a friend of mine, once said, "Witnessing is simply one beggar telling another beggar where to get bread!" If you have found the Bread of Life and are satisfied, how can you keep that Source to yourself?

I think it is obvious that the Word plays an integral part in being born again. So you now understand my reason for believing that "born of water" refers to the Word of God. I also have one more reason for holding this point of view. Look up John 15:3 and Ephesians 5:26, and you'll see that the Word of God is symbolized by water.

Let me ask you one question as we end our time today: Are your feet beautiful in God's eyes? They are if you are sharing His Word and what He has done in you by it with others.

# 13

*B*eing born again is a supernatural act of God that changes a person. Like the wind, you don't see it happen. But again like the wind, you know it has happened because you can see its effect. It is often gradual. Its timing is different—slower in some, faster in others—but it is there. Children grow! If there is no effect, then there has been no genuine birth. Don't be deceived! "No one who is born of God practices sin,[3] because His seed *[sperm]* abides in him; and he cannot sin, because he is born of God. By this the children of God and the children of the devil are obvious: anyone who does not practice righteousness is not of God, nor the one who does not love his brother" (1 John 3:9,10).

It is possible to enter the kingdom of heaven only by being born again. For it is our new birth that changes us, making us new creatures with the indwelling Holy Spirit, who causes us to walk in God's statutes and keep His commandments (Romans 8:1-4; Ezekiel 36:27). In new birth God removes our deceitful heart of stone and gives us a heart of flesh. "Moreover, I will give you a new heart and put a new spirit within you; and I will remove the heart of stone from your flesh and give you a heart of flesh. I will put My Spirit within you and cause you to walk in My statutes, and you will be careful to observe My ordinances" (Ezekiel 36:26,27).

Thus, Paul writes to the Corinthians: "You are our letter, written in our hearts, known and read by all men; being manifested that you are a letter of Christ, cared for by us, written not with ink but with the Spirit of the living God, not on tablets of stone but on tablets of human hearts" (2 Corinthians 3:2,3).

Being born again makes a person an overcomer, as far as sin and the world are concerned.

First John was written "to you who believe in the name of the Son of God, so that you may know that you have eternal life" (1 John 5:13). It is a book that lays before its reader the evidences of being born again, of being a genuine child of God. As in his Gospel, John uses the metaphor "born again" to describe true salvation. "Whoever believes that Jesus is the Christ is born of God, and whoever loves the Father loves the child born of Him. By this we know that we love the children of God, when we love God and observe His commandments. For this is the love of God, that we keep His commandments; and His commandments are not burdensome. For whatever is born of God overcomes the world; and this is the victory that has overcome the world—our faith. Who is the one who overcomes the world, but he who believes that Jesus is the Son of God?" (1 John 5:1-5).

O Beloved, according to God's Word, are you born again?

$14$

$W$hen Jesus told Nicodemus that he must be born of water and of the Spirit if he ever wanted to enter the kingdom of heaven, Nicodemus asked, "How can these things be?" (John 3:9). In other words, "How can this new birth come to pass?"

As we look at the remainder of John 3, we are going to see two ways that the new birth "can be." It can come to pass because of what God did out of love and mercy in lifting up the Son of Man even as Moses lifted up the serpent in the wilderness. Second, it can come to pass because of what we do in response to what God did. Beloved, before we look at this, please take a few minutes and prayerfully read through John 3:7-36.

Man can be born again and enter the kingdom of heaven because of what God did to the Son of Man, the Lord Jesus Christ. "As Moses lifted up the serpent in the wilderness, even so must the Son of Man be lifted up; so that whoever believes will in Him have eternal life" (John 3:14,15).

Do you remember when Moses lifted up the serpent in the wilderness? The account is in Numbers 21. God had brought the children of Israel out of their bondage in Egypt through His mighty power, leading all the way by a pillar of cloud during the day and a pillar of fire at night. As they went, God delivered them from the hands of their enemies, except when they would not fully obey Him.

Yet, for all God's provisions on their journey, they were still discontented. "The people spoke against God and Moses, 'Why have you brought us up out of Egypt to die in the wilderness? For there is no food and no water, and we loathe this miserable food'" (Numbers 21:5).

God gave them manna every morning and provided meat in the form of quail, but nothing could satisfy them. They had cried out in their bondage, and God had delivered them. Now, in even the simpler things, they would not trust God but continually murmured that they were going to die. Finally, God had enough: "The LORD sent fiery serpents among the people and they bit the people, so that many people of Israel died. So the people came to Moses and said, 'We have sinned, because we have spoken against the LORD and you; intercede with the LORD, that He may remove the serpents from us.' And Moses interceded for the people. Then the LORD said to Moses, 'Make a fiery serpent, and set it on a standard; and it shall come about, that everyone who is bitten, when he looks at it, he will live.' And Moses made a bronze serpent and set it on the standard; and it came about, that if a serpent bit any man, when he looked to the bronze serpent, he lived" (Numbers 21:6-9).

It was a look of faith that saved them from death. And for us, it is looking on the One who was made sin for us, and believing that this is the only act of obedient faith which will keep us from perishing. Have you looked to Him in faith's obedience?

## 15

*B*itten and doomed to die because of their sin, the only hope for the children of Israel was to believe God and look at the serpent lifted up in the wilderness. Otherwise, death's certain judgment awaited them. Little did they realize that this serpent on the pole would become a type of the Messiah, the Savior of the world. The Savior who, although He knew no sin, would be made sin for us that we "might become the righteousness of God in Him" (2 Corinthians 5:21).

The serpent on the pole was representative of God's love, for He gave His only begotten Son so that whoever believes in Him, though bitten because of sin, would not perish but have eternal life (John 3:16; see also verses 17-21). Instead of perishing, they would receive everlasting life because they heard and heeded God's Word and were born again, not of corruptible seed, but of the Word of God which lives and abides forever. Hallelujah! Believe! Do what God says!

Those who love evil, who practice it habitually, who hate the Light because it exposes their sin, are not candidates for the kingdom of heaven. However, those who sin but genuinely hate it and long to be set free will look to the Savior hanging on God's tree. As they look with faith's obedience, they will be saved, just as those who looked to the serpent in the wilderness were healed.

In the wilderness, it was trust and obey or die! There is no middle of the road, no safety lane. "He who believes in the Son has eternal life; but he who does not obey the Son will not see life, but the wrath of God abides on him" (John 3:36). The word for *obey* is *peith* and is a present active verb, thereby showing habitual, though not perfect, obedience that comes from persuasion, as a result of genuine faith.

Never let anyone convince you otherwise, Beloved. Genuine faith is seen in its obedience to the Word of God.

# 16

*E*xalting Jesus Christ was John the Baptist's reason for living. He did not follow Jesus Christ to bask in His glory or be noticed as part of Jesus' "intimate circle." John's desire was not to increase his own popularity by his association with Jesus Christ. How rare he was! Even his own disciples could not understand him.

John had been baptizing in Aenon near Salim. When his disciples knew that Jesus "was spending time with them and baptizing...they came to John and said to him, 'Rabbi, He who was with you beyond the Jordan, to whom you have testified, behold, He is baptizing, and all are coming to Him'" (John 3:22,26). It seems, doesn't it, that they were jealous that Jesus was drawing more followers than their teacher, John the Baptist?

This is not a new problem. We begin to measure our success by the number of followers we can draw into our church, our ministry, our group. We want them to be *ours*. We want to build our little kingdom and put a fence around it, so no one can entice away our followers. We get caught up in our own little worlds and miss His world where the harvesters are too few. We don't want our followers to go out into the world as harvesters unless they go out under our flag, so that our ministry gets the glory.

How avaricious our flesh is for glory! How vain! No wonder Jesus warned us to watch and pray, for "the spirit is willing, but the flesh is weak" (Matthew 26:41).

We can learn tremendously valuable lessons from John's response, especially in our time when there is so much promotion of Christian "superstars."

As our ministry has become increasingly well-known, it has been a battle to resist those who want to promote "me." I have also been on guard in my own heart so that I would encourage other ministries similar to ours when possible. I never want to come to a place where I think we have a corner on the truth.

How well I need to remember John's words of wisdom: "A man can receive nothing unless it has been given him from heaven" (John 3:27). Whatever measure of ministry the Lord has so graciously allowed you or me to perform in His vineyard, it truly is a privilege from Him, something for which He has gifted us. As 1 Corinthians 12:4-6 teaches, the gifts, the ministries, and the effects all come from the Godhead. "For from Him and through Him and to Him are all things. To Him be the glory forever. Amen" (Romans 11:36).

May John's sober assessment of life be ours: "He must increase, but I must decrease" (John 3:30). Will you pray for me in this respect, my beloved friend, as I have just prayed for you?

# 17

$\mathcal{H}$e had to pass through Samaria" as surely as He had to leave His Father's ivory palaces and come to earth as a Man. Love drove Him from His heavenly home to earth because man would perish eternally chained to his sin unless the Son of Man came and died in his stead. It was that same love that caused Jesus to pass through Samaria rather than go around it.

The Jews despised the Samaritans. Because they considered them nothing more than dogs, no respectable Jew would sully the sandals on his feet with Samaritan soil. The walk from Jerusalem to Galilee might be shorter if one were to go through Samaria, but it wasn't worth it since the Jews had no dealings with the Samaritans.

Jesus had to pass through Samaria because "she" was there—a woman whose craving for happiness and satisfaction had caused her to drink at many polluted wells, each one leaving her still unsatisfied. As usual, our Lord's timing was perfect. In the heat of the day at high noon, the woman of Samaria put her waterpot on her head and journeyed down the road that led to Jacob's well. I'm sure she chose that time to go for water, for she knew that the women of her city with their forked tongues would not be there. It was painful to hear them chattering as she approached, and then go to whispers as she neared, and then go as silent as the stones once she was in earshot. It was easier to bear the heat of the day than the fire of their condemning eyes.

I imagine the Samaritan woman, like me on the day I met Jesus the Christ, thought it was just another ordinary day. I wonder if she, too, found it hard to get out of bed, to face another day? I wonder if her dreams were sweeter than her life, for in dreams you can be loved by the perfect man; life is as you always hoped and prayed it would be. You can be wildly in love, deliriously happy, ecstatically romantic. My dreams came from the Hollywood productions of the 1940s and 1950s. Hers probably came from the stories passed down from one generation to another, as young and old gathered at wells to chat or as they sat beside fires burning brightly in the night.

My life, like the Samaritan woman's, was a tragedy. It played like a movie you wish you had never seen and read like a novel you don't want to read. It was so sad, so empty, so seemingly pointless. "Why couldn't it have been written with a happy ending?" Life with one lover after another, but never with the one who played the role according to my script.

If the expression was as old as Samaria, I'm sure she too felt, "I've made my bed; now I've got to sleep in it." Little did she know when she rolled out of bed that morning that she wouldn't have to sleep in it any longer. That day Jesus "had to pass through Samaria" (John 4:4).

# 18

*F*rom the day the Samaritan woman met Jesus, she would never be the same. If you have truly met Him, if you have drunk freely of the water that springs up to eternal life, I know you understand what I mean.

Before we go back to this wonderful story in John 4, I hope you will stop and read John 4.

I'll never forget the first time I visited Jacob's well. I went crazy buying every article the Greek Orthodox priest sold! I so related to "the woman at the well," this sinful woman of Samaria, that I bought the crudely shaped wooden plaque bearing the clay form of the Samaritan woman and her water pot sitting on the edge of the well. I also bought the little, brightly painted ceramic replicas of water pots and filled them with the water from Jacob's well.

My treasures were carefully wrapped and brought home, where the plaque was tucked away because it did not fit in my decor. The bottles were given away, but they weren't filled with the water, since it evaporated in the Jerusalem heat.

Although my souvenirs lost their original excitement, never again will I read John 4 without seeing the whole setting in my mind. Never will I forget where I sat in the garden outside the little grotto-like structure erected around Jacob's well, looking at Mount Gerizim and Mount Ebal and thinking what it must have been like for my

Samaritan friend to walk to that well every day, passing between these two mountains.

Mount Gerizim was the mount of blessing; Ebal was the mount of cursing. These were the mountains where Joshua had the priests stand and read the blessings and the cursings of the Old Covenant: blessings if they obeyed God and cursings if they did not! (Joshua 8:33,34).

Surely those cursings resounded off Mount Ebal as my Samaritan friend passed under its shadow day in and day out. Surely the barrenness of that mountain, in comparison to Gerizim, reminded her of the barrenness of her own life because she had not heeded the words given earlier by Moses: "I call heaven and earth to witness against you today, that I have set before you life and death, the blessing and the curse. So choose life in order that you may live, you and your descendants, by loving the LORD your God, by obeying His voice, and by holding fast to Him; for this is your life and the length of your days, that you may live in the land which the LORD swore to your fathers, to Abraham, Isaac, and Jacob, to give them" (Deuteronomy 30:19,20).

O Beloved, do you live in the shadow of a mountain of curses because you have failed to obey God? Or have you drunk of Him and never been the same?

# $19$

$D$o you know someone like the Samaritan woman—who has obviously messed up his or her life? Have you ever approached that one with the good news of the gospel of Jesus Christ? Probably many of you would say, "No!" Probably it's "no" because you just wouldn't know how to approach such a person. As a matter of fact, if you are a typical Christian, witnessing to anyone is not the easiest thing in the world to do, unless God has given you the spiritual gift of evangelism.

Well, Beloved, not having the gift of evangelism does not let you or me off the hook when it comes to sharing the gospel of Jesus Christ! This is the duty of every child of God. Paul wrote, "I am under obligation both to Greeks and to barbarians, both to the wise and to the foolish. So, for my part, I am eager to preach the gospel" (Romans 1:14,15). We are to "preach the word," to "be ready in season and out of season" (2 Timothy 4:2), for "faith comes from hearing, and hearing by the word of Christ" (Romans 10:17), and "how will they hear without a preacher?" (Romans 10:14).

In the light of our obligation and of the desperate plight of those enslaved to sin, as even once we were, let's see what we can learn from John 4 and the way our Lord presented the gospel to this needy woman.

I believe the most common method of evangelism, and probably one of the most effective and biblical means of evangelism, is what Dr. Joe Aldrich, former president of Multnomah School of the Bible, terms "lifestyle evangelism." The premise of lifestyle evangelism, as I understand it, is that sharing the gospel is a natural outflow of your life as you are in contact with those who do not know Jesus Christ. It does not mean that you "buttonhole" everyone you meet and share the gospel with them. Rather, it means that your sharing of Jesus Christ is a natural outflow of your life. You share as you go with any you come into contact with, in a daily walk ordered under the lordship of Jesus Christ.

Stop and pray about this concept. Are you sharing the gospel at all, Beloved? We'll discuss it some more tomorrow.

# 20

"$G$oing from door to door, passing out tracts, and asking people if they are saved just isn't for me!" Are those your sentiments? I understand. Don't feel guilty. There are many who feel this way. While this is an effective means of evangelism for some, I do not believe it is for everyone. Nor do I believe you will see it taught in the Scriptures as "the way" to evangelize.

That ought to enable many of you to breathe a sigh of relief. However, it does not let you off the proverbial hook when it comes to your responsibility to the lost. As I understand the Scriptures, lifestyle evangelism is the responsibility of every Christian. And I don't think one of us can escape our responsibility. Jesus said, "You are the salt of the earth" (Matthew 5:13).

Salt does three things. It brings out the flavor of food. Your life ought to bring forth the flavor of Christ. Second, salt stops the spread of corruption. Your life of righteousness ought to have that effect among your associates and associations. Third, salt causes a person to thirst. Does your life make others thirsty for the One you have and the changes Jesus brings?

Matthew not only tells you that you are salt, he also points out that "you are the light of the world." So "let your light shine before men in such a way that they may see your good works, and glorify your Father who is in heaven" (Matthew 5:14,16). Living "in the midst of a crooked and perverse generation, among whom you appear as lights in the world, holding fast the word of life" (Philippians 2:15,16) puts you in the position for lifestyle evangelism. Thus, you are able to fulfill Matthew 28:19,20: "Go therefore and make disciples of all the nations [in other words, don't exclude anyone because of their nationality or religious persuasion]...teaching them to observe all that I commanded you; and lo, I am with you always, even to the end of the age." The main command is "make disciples"; the other verbs are all participles. Therefore, it could be translated, "Make disciples... baptizing...teaching."

This is a natural evangelism, a lifestyle evangelism which takes the pressure and guilt off of sharing the gospel. This lifestyle enables you to make witnessing a natural outflow of sharing the One who lives within with those He brings into your path. You speak to those the Spirit of God says to speak to!

Isn't this what we see in John 4? Jesus had to go through Samaria—the Spirit of God was leading Him. As He went, He shared.

You see the same type of incident in John 3. Jesus was in Jerusalem, led by the Spirit. Nicodemus, who saw the lifestyle of Jesus and was attracted to Him, came to Him at night because he knew Jesus was from God. And Jesus gave Nicodemus what he had been searching for—the way to be sure you have eternal life.

Do people come to you? Do you share by your life and as the Spirit leads with those who are in your days? If not, why not?

# 21

$\mathcal{I}$s there a formula for sharing the gospel? Is there a particular way you can share so that you'll see results most of the time? As you look at Jesus' lifestyle evangelism, and as you compare John 3 and John 4, you find that our Lord dealt with Nicodemus and the Samaritan woman differently!

Although there is no pat way to share the gospel when you witness, you must make sure that it is the gospel you share and not just your "sweet" story or your "exciting" conversion.

Our goal for today is to see how Jesus ministered the gospel to those with whom the Father brought Him into contact. There are some precious and valuable insights which will help you, Beloved. Why don't you stop and ask God to really minister to you? He loves to have you seek His face!

If you are going to witness, then you need to be in contact with those who are lost! Exposure is of primary importance in witnessing. There is a mentality among some Christians that we ought to stay as far away from "the world" as possible. As a result, some find themselves so involved in Christian activities—living in Christian communes, taking Christian vacations, and working in Christian organizations—that the world never has a chance to see their lifestyle.

Do you have any exposure to lost people at all? One of the things you find Jesus doing, although He was criticized for it, was spending time with lost people.

The Pharisees were horrified when Jesus went to Matthew's home and ate with many tax-gatherers and sinners. When they asked Jesus' disciples, "Why is your Teacher eating with the tax collectors and sinners?" Jesus said, "It is not those who are healthy who need a physician, but those who are sick. But go and learn what this means, 'I DESIRE COMPASSION, AND NOT SACRIFICE,' for I did not come to call the righteous, but sinners" (Matthew 9:11-13).

Sinners had access to our Lord. Do they have access to you? Do they even know you exist? Do they have a chance to see your good works, to watch your lifestyle enough so that they ask you to give a reason "for the hope that is in you" (1 Peter 3:15)?

Jesus went through Samaria purposefully. He stayed at the well when His disciples went to get something to eat. Jesus knew she would be there! Ours, Beloved, is a "go" gospel—go into the world because there we will find those who are lost and need to be found.

Have you thought of beginning each day by making yourself available to the Father so that your life might be a witness to those He wants to touch through you? Try it—see what happens.

# 22

*W*hen you witness, it is best to meet people where they are, rather than with a tract or an immediate presentation of the gospel. Of course, the way you meet an individual will depend on circumstances and the time you have. As far as we know, Jesus had only one opportunity to talk with both Nicodemus and the Samaritan woman. Yet, His approach with each was different.

With Nicodemus, Jesus moved into the subject of salvation immediately. Of course, Nicodemus was interested, and Jesus knew that by his question; and since Nicodemus was a Pharisee, his life was invested in spiritual matters. Jesus knew why Nicodemus had come.

However, with the woman at the well, it was another story. Her interest was water. So Jesus met her there. Let's watch how Jesus dealt with her and see what He did so that we might use the same principles in our witnessing.

Take a few minutes and read through John 4 from the perspective of witnessing, and then list your insights in your notebook. It will make a difference for you if you dig these truths out on your own before you learn them from someone else. As you read John 4, list what you learn from the way Jesus dealt with this lost woman. And if you have extra time, try the same thing for Nicodemus in John 3:1-21. We'll talk more tomorrow!

# 23

$\mathcal{A}$s I have studied the Word, I have learned much that has helped me in sharing the gospel. Because of the lifestyle to which God has called me, I really do not have time for long-term, intimate friendships with people who are lost. Jack and I live right on the conference grounds of Precept Ministries; therefore, we do not have any close associations with neighbors. Plus, as heads of a ministry, our lives are extremely busy in dealing with a staff of 120-plus, with those who come to our various programs and conferences, and also with those we meet as we travel. Therefore, most of our witnessing is done when we are "on the road."

However, what I have learned from studying John 3 and 4 and other segments of the Word has helped me greatly. So let me share from John 3 and 4, and see how it compares with what you saw. If you are going to share the gospel, you need contact with those who are lost.

Sometimes people will come to you as Nicodemus did to Jesus. Or, if you are dealing with a long-term associate or friend, then you may find your friend coming to you for help with a problem or simply asking you about the difference in your life. In this case, your walk with Christ has opened the door, and you are ready to move in. How? This is what Joe Aldrich shares in his fascinating and inspiring book *Life-Style Evangelism.* You will have to read it. It is absolutely super!

At other times, you will find yourself in the path of someone you don't even know. What do you do then? Well, the first thing I do is to ask God if He wants me to share, and if He does, to open the door or to show me how to open it.

Jesus opens the conversation with the Samaritan woman by asking her for a drink. He focuses on a subject that is appropriate to the occasion and centers on her immediate interests. From there, Jesus will turn the conversation to salvation, to show her how it will benefit her.

He does the same thing with Nicodemus, explaining that if Nicodemus is born again, he will see the kingdom of heaven. This was what every Pharisee wanted!

What do you see Jesus doing as He presents the gospel? First, there is contact. Then He relates the truth of the Word of God to where the person is.

O Beloved, learn the Word so you can relate it to any need or question of man. Begin by scratching people where they itch! Thus they'll be more eager to listen.

*24*

When you share the gospel, it is vital that you do not get sidetracked on controversial issues which would keep the lost from even hearing what they need to hear. Avoid arguments. Don't get tied up in the nonessentials. Remember, a lost person cannot even begin to comprehend the things of God apart from the Spirit of God.

Jesus totally avoided the woman's retort that Jews had no dealings with Samaritans. Also, He did not debate with her about which mountain was the true mountain from which to worship. Instead of getting caught up in controversy, Jesus engaged her attention by talking about things she was interested in. He related what He said to spiritual matters: "Whoever drinks of the water that I will give him shall never thirst; but the water that I will give him will become in him a well of water springing up to eternal life" (John 4:14). When she asked for the water, Jesus confronted her with her sin. You see the same thing in Jesus' dealing with Nicodemus when He confronted him with his unbelief (John 3:11,12).

When you share the gospel, you must confront the lost with their sin. Christ came to save sinners. The issue of sin must be dealt with because only salvation can deliver them from sin. This, Beloved, is where repentance enters. People see their sin, then repent, then believe.

Jesus confronted the Samaritan woman with her sin by asking her to call her husband. There has been many a time, as I have prayerfully shared the gospel, when God has caused me to ask a specific question in order to bring a person face-to-face with his or her sin. At this point, the conversation can become very touchy. However, if I confront in love, if I share how I was a slave to sin before I came to know Jesus Christ, then the person sees my genuine concern and is not offended as his or her sin is exposed.

There are three more points I want to share to help you in sharing the gospel. First, make sure people see that salvation is by faith, not by works. Jesus brings this out in John 4:21-24 and 3:13-15. Second, when you share, remember in salvation the issue is, "What will you do with Jesus?" Do not get sidetracked! And finally, don't push salvation. Give the Holy Spirit time to convict. Only God can give the increase. So don't pick green fruit! He is the Lord of the harvest. You just make sure your meat is to do the will of Him who sent you. Then get out into those fields which are white (overripe) unto harvest. You won't be sorry (unless, of course, you don't go)!

# Taking Action and Walking by Faith

## John 5–7

# 25

*I*f you could see signs and wonders and miracles, would it make a difference in the way you respond to God and to His Word? The Jews kept asking to see signs. Yet many who saw Jesus perform them still did not believe that He was the Christ, the Son of God. It is no wonder that Jesus became weary with them and said, "Unless you people see signs and wonders, you simply will not believe" (John 4:48).

For many, one sign is seldom good enough. How deceitful and desperately wicked is the heart of a man or woman who does not know Jesus! To recognize Him for who He is would be to acknowledge that He is God, and man wants to be his own god. He doesn't want to submit to anyone or anything but his own desires, his own ambitions.

Jesus was born to die for your sins and mine. Yet before He died, He performed many signs so that we might know beyond a shadow of a doubt that He truly was the Christ sent to be "the Lamb of God who takes away the sin of the world!" (John 1:29).

As we continue our devotional study of the first 11 chapters of the Gospel of John, we will look at a select number of signs recorded by the apostle John which "have been written so that you may believe that Jesus is the Christ, the Son of God; and that believing you may have life in His name" (John 20:31). O Beloved, my prayer for you is that your mind and heart may be so taken captive by the truths recorded in the Gospel of John that you will not need to see signs but may be able to walk in faith, taking God at His word. I pray you will walk by faith and not by sight "having been firmly rooted and now being built up in Him and established in your faith" (Colossians 2:7).

As we move through the first 11 chapters of John, we behold various signs which prove beyond a shadow of a doubt who Jesus is. And as we carefully scrutinize His life, we come to know our heavenly Father in a new dimension. We see Jesus as "the only begotten God who is in the bosom of the Father" who came to explain Him (John 1:18), for those who have seen Jesus have seen the Father (John 14:9).

As you spend time in this Gospel each day, it is my prayer that your Savior will become your dear, dear Friend.

# 26

"Do you wish to get well?" It seems like a rather foolish question on the surface! At first you think, "Who wouldn't wish to get well?"

I ask these questions, and my mind races to a man sitting at one of the gates surrounding the Old City of Jerusalem. As I recently came out of the Old City into the noise of lumbering buses jammed to the doors with Arabs and to the honking of irate, impassioned cab drivers, as I felt the bright sunshine which had been shielded by the walled, crowded, narrow streets of the Old City, a man sitting on the ground caught my attention. He was happily conversing with other beggars until a foreign tourist came by. At that point, all conversation ceased, and a hand was lifted as dark eyes silently pled for alms. The other hand pulled up a pant leg to make sure the already exposed ulcer— bright pink, glazed over with white purulent patches glistening in the sun—was not missed.

My nurse's heart brought my feet to a halt. I wanted to bend down and shield the open wound from the dust sent flying by the traffic scurrying through the gate. His leg needed tending. It should be washed, medicated, and dressed by someone who cared. Why, unattended it would only eat away until it reached his bone, and then he could lose his leg!

Arrested by his plight, I stopped to gaze at his leg and look into the darkness of his eyes, until my friend gently took me by my elbow and propelled me toward our destination. I was a tourist and did not know about these things. She then proceeded to tell me that this man did not wish to be made well. He made his living from his wound. No need to confront the complexities of responsibility as a citizen of Israel when one could merely sit down in the dust and dirt of Jerusalem and receive pity along with a few shekels.

My wounded beggar could have been healed. The hospital doors were open to him and medicine was available, but he did not wish to get well. As I looked back in curious fascination, I caught one last glimpse of someone less than what he could have been.

The man in John 5 had been sick for 38 years. We do not know how long he had been lying beside the pool of Bethesda. All we know is that when Jesus passed by and asked him if he wished to be made well, he had to make a choice. Either he could continue in his normal habit of life, or he could relinquish it for healing.

Suppose, Beloved, Jesus asked you if you wanted to be made well emotionally, physically, spiritually? What would you answer? Think about it, read John 5, and we'll talk about it more tomorrow.

## 27

*H*ave you ever blamed your condition on what others have not done for you? Maybe you have been greatly hurt or disappointed, and you feel crippled, as if you can't live the way you want to. You think of what you might have been, if only you hadn't suffered so.

Do you understand, Beloved, what I am saying? It could mean wholeness to you and a new lease on life. If you relate to what I just said, then you can relate to the certain man of John 5 who had been crippled for 38 years. "But," you may say, "I am not physically crippled." Granted. But physically crippled or emotionally handicapped because of what has happened to you, the underlying precept is still the same.

The infirm man had a problem similar to that of many people today: He was resigned to his infirmity. That is why Jesus asked him if he wished to get well. Jesus knew his heart and looked beneath the outward circumstances to the inward condition. The man's answer gives us insight into his real condition: "Sir, I have no man to put me into the pool when the water is stirred up, but while I am coming, another steps down before me" (John 5:7).

I think of people who are sick in the sense that they are not whole, people with wounds that have come from relationships with others, wounds that have never been tended and healed. Wounds that could be healed if the person stopped blaming another for the condition and acted in faith; wounds that could be healed if he had stopped his self-pity and dull acceptance of the infirmity and moved to the obedience of faith.

The infirm man of John 5 had to take action. Jesus told him to rise, take up his pallet, and walk. If he really wanted to be made whole, he had to stop blaming others. No more lying around apathetic, resigned to his state, saying, "I am what I am; I am where I am; and I will always be here because others have failed me." He needed to believe Jesus and get up and go on with life.

Beloved, there is a balm in Gilead. It is the Word of God (Psalm 107:20). There is a Great Physician there. It is God our Healer, our Jehovah-Rapha (Exodus 15:26). Cry out, "Heal me, O LORD, and I will be healed; save me and I will be saved, for You are my praise" (Jeremiah 17:14).

# 28

Sin has an awful price. It can affect every aspect of our being—physically, emotionally, spiritually. It is interesting that Jesus said to the man who had been in his sickness 38 years, "Behold, you have become well; do not sin anymore, so that nothing worse happens to you" (John 5:14). So many times we think of sin as gross acts. Yet according to the Scriptures, the root of all sin is independence from God. In the Garden of Eden, Adam and Eve chose to disobey God's word and to seek their own good.

In Romans 14:23, we read: "Whatever is not from faith is sin." Therefore, not to believe God's Word and to live independently of what He says is sin. Often the people who ask me for counseling fall into two categories: Some say, "I know God's Word says that, *but,* you see, in my case it is different." Then there are those who say, "If that is what God's Word says, then I am going to live accordingly, no matter how I feel."

It is the latter group, Beloved, who are healed, made whole, and are useful to the kingdom of heaven. They take action and begin to walk in the victory of faith. Not to be made whole or well, emotionally or spiritually, is sin. It is to refuse to believe God. And when we do this, even greater woes may befall us.

You may feel that I am avoiding the issue of physical healing. Therefore, let me explain. I believe that God can and does heal physical illnesses today. However, I do not believe that the Scriptures teach that physical healing is for everyone in every situation.

It is interesting to me that in John 5 there was "a multitude of…sick, blind, lame, and withered" people lying around the pool called Bethesda (verse 3). Yet we see Jesus healed only one of them. There was no mass healing service. Why? Obviously, mass healing did not serve the purpose of our sovereign God.

I believe that sometimes God heals people to bring Himself glory and sometimes He allows a child of God to endure physical illness for His glory.

However, for a child of God to be emotionally or spiritually crippled because of the past is not scriptural. The Word promises us that "God causes all things to work together for good to those who love God, to those who are called according to His purpose. For those whom He foreknew, He also predestined to become conformed to the image of His Son" (Romans 8:28,29). Be healed, Beloved.

## 29

*H*ave you ever known people who boxed God into the confines of their own legalism? Who defined holiness and Christianity according to a set of rules or traditions or commandments which they themselves ordained? The Pharisees did this. They took the clear teachings of the Word of God and added to them dos and don'ts that would keep the Jews from even coming close to breaking the commandments of the Old Testament.

The Jews added rules to what God said about the Sabbath. In Exodus 20, God said: "Remember the sabbath day, to keep it holy. Six days you shall labor and do all your work, but the seventh day is a sabbath of the LORD your God; in it you shall not do any work, you or your son or your daughter, your male or your female servant or your cattle or your sojourner who stays with you. For in six days the LORD made the heavens and the earth, the sea and all that is in them, and rested on the seventh day; therefore the LORD blessed the sabbath day and made it holy" (20:8-11).

On the seventh day, "even during plowing time and harvest you shall rest" (Exodus 34:21). To break the Sabbath meant death. God's word through Moses was clear: It was to be "a sabbath of complete rest to the LORD; whoever does any work on it shall be put to death. You shall not kindle a fire in any of your dwellings on the sabbath day" (Exodus 35:2,3).

Death for breaking the Sabbath was not merely an ordinance written in the book of the Law and never executed. Numbers 15 records an incident of a man gathering wood on the Sabbath day: "Those who found him gathering wood brought him to Moses and Aaron and to all the congregation; and they put him in custody because it had not been declared what should be done to him. Then the Lord said to Moses, 'The man shall surely be put to death; all the congregation shall stone him with stones outside the camp.' So all the congregation brought him outside the camp and stoned him to death with stones, just as the Lord had commanded Moses" (15:33-36).

It was because of the gravity of breaking the Law that the Jews built a hedge of protection around it with their codification of the Law. Their reasoning was that if their people kept these traditions, then there was no way they could come close to transgressing God's Law.

Though their intentions may have been good, these Jews came to consider man-made traditions equal with the Law. Therefore, they considered disobedience of these punishable with the same punishment meted out for disobeying the Law. In their good intentions, they added to the Word of God. How dangerous and how crippling! Their legalism so blinded them that they missed who Jesus was. Have you missed Him or His grace because of your legalism?

# 30

*R*esisting another's legalistic interpretation of Scripture often brings persecution. How hard it is when this comes from those who profess to have the same heavenly Father. Until He healed the man at the pool of Bethesda, things had gone fairly smoothly in the ministry of our Lord. Merrill Tenney calls the time preceding John 5 "the period of consideration."[4]

However, when He healed this man, Jesus entered into a period of controversy which began in Judea but exacerbated in Galilee. The controversy came from His own people, the Jews.

The primary source of contention was the Pharisees' claim that Abraham was their father, allowing them also to claim God as their Father (John 8:39-41). They saw themselves as the protectors and interpreters of the Law. The Pharisees occupied the majority of the seats in the Sanhedrin which, under Rome, was the ruling body over the Jews.

This period of controversy in Jesus' public ministry was inaugurated because Jesus healed the man on the Sabbath. The Jews said to the man, "'It is the Sabbath, and it is not permissible for you to carry your pallet.' But he answered them, 'He who made me well was the one who said to me, "Pick up your pallet and walk."'...For this reason the Jews were persecuting Jesus, because He was doing these things on the Sabbath" (John 5:10-11,16).

Over and over, we see Jesus healing on the Sabbath. That interests me! He could have healed on another day of the week, but He didn't choose to. When our Lord healed on the Sabbath, He exposed the degree to which their legalism had become twisted.

Sometimes people today get so caught up in their legalistic understanding of Christianity that they miss what God is doing, or they seek to stifle it.

O Beloved, don't let it happen to you! Watch that you don't persecute or demean other children of God just because they don't fit your religious mold. You may be resisting the work of God.

# 31

$\mathcal{A}$s we move into adulthood, we want to be free to make our own decisions, to answer to ourselves rather than to others. This desire is part of the maturing process. And yet, independence must not spill over into our walk with our Lord.

The secret of spirituality, of being used of God, is dependence, not independence. Never is this truth more beautifully or powerfully illustrated for us than in the relationship of our Lord Jesus Christ to His heavenly Father. I want us to look at this relationship in detail, for in it we learn invaluable insights that need to be incorporated into our own lives.

It was the very relationship Christ claimed with the Father which heightened the controversy between the Jews and Jesus. When they questioned Jesus' healing of the man on the Sabbath, He answered them, "'My Father is working until now, and I Myself am working.' For this reason therefore the Jews were seeking all the more to kill Him, because He not only was breaking the Sabbath, but also was calling God His own Father, making Himself equal with God" (John 5:17,18). To make oneself equal to God or claim to be God falsely was considered blasphemy, and the Word of God said that blasphemy was punishable by death.

To explain why He healed the man on the Sabbath, Jesus answered, "Truly, truly, I say to you, the Son can do nothing of Himself, unless it is something He sees the Father doing; for whatever the Father does, these things the Son also does in like manner" (John 5:19). Jesus healed the man on the Sabbath because that was the pleasure of His Father. In total dependence upon the Father, Jesus executed God's desire.

And in doing so, He modeled for us how we are to live as children of God. As we live more and more in total dependence upon the Father, we will become more and more like Jesus.

And to be like Jesus, dear child of God, is the whole reason for our existence and life upon this earth!

To be like Jesus, we must learn to walk as Christ walked with His Father, doing nothing on our own initiative. May it be our habit of life to "always do the things that are pleasing to Him" (John 8:29), and to be mature enough to not live independently of Him but in total dependence.

# 32

$I$s it possible to live in total dependence upon the Father? Yes! Our Lord Jesus Christ lived that way because He lived by the Spirit. We too are to be controlled or filled by the Spirit.

You may say to me, "But, Kay, Jesus was God!" Yes, Beloved, Jesus is God. However, when He lived here on earth as the Son of Man, He lived as God always intended man to live—in complete dependence upon Him and His Word. To live in dependence is to walk in the Spirit. Dependence upon the Father dictates that we live by faith, taking God at His Word.

In Genesis 3, man sinned when he "turned to his own way" (Isaiah 53:6), when he ceased to believe and submit to God, when he chose not to do what God commanded. It was at this point that the Spirit of God left man, and man passed from life into death (Romans 5:12). And it is not until man passes from death to life that he is saved.

And how does salvation affect man's relationship to the Spirit of God? "He saved us, not on the basis of deeds...but according to His mercy, by the washing of regeneration and renewing by the Holy Spirit, whom He poured out upon us richly through Jesus Christ our Savior" (Titus 3:5,6).

Jesus lived and walked by the same Spirit who indwells every believer. Jesus modeled for us what God intended for man when He created him. Thus, we see Jesus beginning His ministry with "the Spirit descending and remaining upon Him" (John 1:33), the same Spirit with whom He shall baptize every believer at salvation (1 Corinthians 12:13). This is the same Holy Spirit who indwells us, who leads us, who guides us into all truth. It is the Spirit of God who "searches all things, even the depths of God" and then makes them known unto us so that we have the mind of Christ (1 Corinthians 2:10-16).

Now then, Beloved, let us return to John 5, where Jesus defined His dependence upon the Father. "The Son can do nothing of Himself, unless it is something He sees the Father doing; for whatever the Father does, these things the Son also does in like manner. For the Father loves the Son, and shows Him all things that He Himself is doing" (John 5:19,20).

A life of dependence upon the Father begins when we become "children of God" (John 1:12), for then the Spirit of God indwells us and reveals to us the mind of God, so that we know what pleases Him. We learn His heart. Then we must choose to do what God has shown us. Jesus said, "I do nothing on My own initiative, but I speak these things as the Father taught Me" (John 8:28). We too are to speak the things the Father teaches us—and do the things He has taught us, the things which please Him.

Now then, Beloved, "the one who says he abides in Him ought himself to walk in the same manner as He walked" (1 John 2:6).

# 33

*J*esus claimed nothing less for Himself than deity. He demanded nothing less from His followers than obedient faith."⁵ In today's portion of John 5, Jesus addresses both of these issues.

In John 5:18, we find the Jews seeking to kill Jesus "because He not only was breaking the Sabbath, but also was calling God His own Father, making Himself equal with God." As Jesus answered them, He showed them that He, like the Father, possessed the sovereign rights of deity.

The first sovereign right of deity is authority over life and death. Deuteronomy 32:39 says, "See now that I, I am He, and there is no god besides Me; it is I who put to death and give life." In John 5:25-27, Jesus points out to the Jews that "an hour is coming and now is, when the dead will hear the voice of the Son of God, and those who hear will live. For just as the Father has life in Himself, even so He gave to the Son also to have life in Himself; and He gave Him authority to execute judgment, because He is the Son of Man."

Jesus' statements lay clear claim to His equality with the Father. Then He speaks of those He will call forth on that day. Jesus now spells out what life in the Spirit produces.

Those who are truly saved follow Him (John 10). It is a life that follows Jesus Christ that produces good deeds. Good works follow salvation and show our faith to be genuine (James 2:14-26). As Jesus says in the Sermon on the Mount, "So then, you will know them by their fruits" (Matthew 7:20).

Genuine salvation will produce good works. Listen to Jesus' words: "Do not marvel at this; for an hour is coming, in which all who are in the tombs will hear His voice, and will come forth; those who did the good deeds to a resurrection of life, those who committed the evil deeds to a resurrection of judgment" (John 5:28,29).

Jesus is not teaching that good works save us. Rather, He is saying that those who possess salvation, eternal life, do good deeds. Our works illustrate our character. Men made righteous produce righteous deeds. Think on these things, Beloved.

*34*

Not only does a sovereign God have power over death and life so that He can raise the dead, but He also has the authority to judge. Judgment is another sovereign right of God. God is "the Judge of all the earth" (Genesis 18:25). Thus, in John 5, Jesus also substantiates His deity by telling the Jews that the Father "gave Him authority to execute judgment, because He is the Son of Man" (5:27). God the Father "has given all judgment to the Son" (5:22).

Not only is judgment the sovereign right of God, God is the Creator, the Sustainer. Thus, Jesus states, "For just as the Father has life in Himself, even so He gave to the Son also to have life in Himself" (John 5:26). "For just as the Father raises the dead and gives them life, even so the Son also gives life to whom He wishes" (John 5:21).

Finally, the last sovereign right of God in this chapter is the right to receive honor. All are to "honor the Son, even as they honor the Father" (John 5:23). If Jesus were not God, then God would not give His glory to Him (Isaiah 42:8).

With all these statements, Jesus is claiming nothing less than deity for Himself. But is Jesus' witness true? Would His testimony of His deity stand alone in the Jews' court of justice? No, and Jesus knows it, for He says, "If I alone testify about Myself, My testimony is not true" (John 5:31) or admissible as legal evidence.

Therefore, in John 5, Jesus lays before the Jews other witnesses who will testify that His witness to His deity is true. What are these witnesses? Well, I want you to find out for yourself by reading John 5:31-47. When you dig out truth on your own, it stays with you. As you read, note every use of the word *witness*. Then list in your notebook those things or people who bear witness to Jesus' deity.

There are many who claim to belong to God and seek to have you join their churches; yet when you get down to the issue of the deity of Jesus Christ, you find that they believe Jesus was a good man, a god, but not God incarnate (in the flesh).

Now then, Beloved, should someone question you, would you be able to share that which bears witness to the fact that Jesus Christ is God?

# 35

$I$sn't it amazing how a person can be confronted with truth after truth, one truth substantiating and confirming the other, and still refuse to believe? Yet the same person is so quick to buy a lie! To be deceived! Have you ever wondered why? It is because men's hearts are deceitful and desperately wicked. Therefore, they love darkness rather than light, and will not come to the light lest their deeds be exposed (John 3:19,20). "The god of this world has blinded the minds of the unbelieving so that they might not see the light of the gospel of the glory of Christ, who is the image of God" (2 Corinthians 4:4). Thus, as it says in John 5:40, "You are unwilling to come to Me so that you may have life."

The Jews had ample witnesses. The Father bore witness of His Son through His word to John the Baptist, through the works which He accomplished through His Son, and sometimes when He spoke audibly from heaven about Jesus.

Finally, the Word of God itself bore witness to Jesus Christ. How I love Jesus' words: "'O foolish men and slow of heart to believe in all that the prophets have spoken!'…Then beginning with Moses and with all the prophets, He explained to them the things concerning Himself in all the Scriptures" (Luke 24:25,27). These were the Scriptures the Jews searched because they thought that in them they had eternal life, and it was these that bore witness of Jesus (John 5:39).

If they searched the Scriptures looking for eternal life, then why did they miss it? They thought for sure that heaven was their destination. However, as you read through John 5:37-47, you see the "negatives" in their lives that would send them to hell. They were men who had never heard the voice of God at any time nor seen His form (John 5:37); yet they would not listen to Jesus, the One who had heard and seen God.

They would not accept His witness. Second, they did not have God's Word abiding in them (John 5:38). They knew the Word backward and forward, but it wasn't at home in them. Third, they were unwilling to come to Jesus that they might have life (John 5:40). And, as Jesus would say later, "No one comes to the Father but through Me" (John 14:6). Fourth, they did not have the love of God in themselves (John 5:42). Fifth, they were quick to receive others, but they did not receive Jesus. Isn't that the same with so many people today? They are quick to believe other books, other opinions, but not the Bible. Sixth, they sought glory from one another, but not from God. Men love the praise of men more than the praise of God. And finally, they wouldn't believe Moses. If they had, they would have believed Jesus, for Moses wrote about Him. It is the same today in the "school of higher criticism," which denies the literal veracity of God's Word. O Beloved, may you not identify with these "negatives" in any way!

# 36

*H*ave you ever walked out of the door of your private, secure world and taken a good look at the outside world around you? Has your heart ever been moved to compassion? Have you ever wondered what you could do to meet the needs of the multitude? We live in a time of great apathy. For the most part, we are a self-centered generation. When a person turns his or her focus on self, apathy follows.

However, I don't believe I am writing to the typical Christian. I don't believe that you would have such an interest in the Word of God if you were, shall I say, ordinary. Typical. Run-of-the-mill. Someone who reads and uses a devotional like this is hungering to know God better. Such a one has a desire to understand the Word of God, and a passion for godliness, holiness, for greater intimacy with God.

Therefore, when I ask if you have ever taken a good look at the world around you and been moved to compassion, I believe you probably have. I don't think you are simply wrapped up in your own private world.

Yet when you look at the world, are you ever overwhelmed? When you look at the state of affairs in your country, when you look at morality, at what is going on in the schools, at what is happening in the homes of your friends, in their marriages, in their children, are you overwhelmed? Do you feel like someone needs to do something? Do you wonder where that someone is?

Well, let me ask you a question, Beloved. Have you ever thought that maybe you were that someone? *Me!* Did I hear you say, *"Me!"* with an incredulous gasp? I understand.

You think, "I have so little to offer." Or, "The need is so overwhelming. Who could ever begin to make a difference?" Or, "I am not prepared for this. I have so little in the way of talents, gifts, capabilities, or time. There's no way I could ever... Why, it would take..."

Hang on, Beloved. A change could be coming if you listen carefully to what God is about to show you through His Word, if you have a soft and tender heart of flesh and not of stone. Keeping in mind what you have just read, now turn to the infallible Word of God and read John 6:1-14; Matthew 14:13-21; Mark 6:30-44; and Luke 9:10-17.

Since all four Gospels record the same event, there has to be great significance to it. And there are surely some principles that are applicable to your life. Ask God to speak to you. Then write down your insights in your notebook.

# 37

$\mathcal{T}$hey were an excited multitude, for they were seeing things they had never seen. Many had come from great distances, walking the dusty roads of Galilee. The news had spread like a brush fire. More than 5000 men, along with women and children, had converged on Jesus. When they looked out on that small Sea of Galilee and saw where He was headed, they took off, literally running on foot from their towns. Jesus went by boat to a desolate place to be alone with His disciples; but when He saw the multitude, like sheep without a shepherd, He had compassion on them.

Jesus spent the day teaching them about the kingdom of God and healing their sick. And although the hour grew late and they had made no prior provision for food or lodging, I am sure they thought, "Why go home?" They might miss something! Besides, it was a lovely time of year. It was Nisan, the beginning of months. Spring had arrived! It was time once again to celebrate the Passover.

The multitude didn't seem concerned, but the disciples were. They came to Jesus saying, "This place is desolate and the hour is already late; so send the crowds away, that they may go into the villages and buy food for themselves" (Matthew 14:15). Can you imagine their shock when Jesus replied, "They do not need to go away; you give them something to eat!" (Matthew 14:16)?

Can you relate to how the disciples must have felt? Here were 5000 hungry men, not counting the women and children. Feed them?

Philip analyzed the situation immediately. It was impossible! Why, it would take two-thirds of a year's wages to feed this mob! That's 200 denarii! It wouldn't be sufficient "for everyone to receive a little" (John 6:7). Of course, we know that Jesus was testing Philip to see if he would look beyond the impossibility of the situation to the God of the Impossible, the One who had just asked him, "Where are we to buy bread, so that these may eat?" (John 6:5).

Isn't that our problem so often, Beloved? We find ourselves over-whelmed by a seemingly impossible need, and we forget to look to God. We forget His word to His people: "Behold, I am the LORD, the God of all flesh; is anything too difficult for Me?" (Jeremiah 32:27). "Call to Me and I will answer you, and I will tell you great and mighty things, which you do not know" (Jeremiah 33:3).

To which we ought to reply: "Ah Lord GOD! Behold, You have made the heavens and the earth by Your great power and by Your outstretched arm! Nothing is too difficult for You" (Jeremiah 32:17). But sometimes we, like Philip, forget to look beyond natural resources to the supernatural. Talk to your God about your feelings.

# 38

*D*o you ever feel that you have a little faith, but not enough? You see a need, you look at what you have or at what you are and it seems inadequate, so you don't do anything. I understand. As far as natural talents, ability, education, and personality, I am just not a winner. You may respond, "But you write books, have a radio program, a television program, you write inductive Bible study courses, and travel all over the world teaching the Bible. I disagree with you." I don't think I am being modest. I just don't feel talented naturally.

All of my 29 years as a lost person, I tried to be a winner. I worked hard, but I never really made it. I studied like mad and could not get above a 92 average. I wanted to be part of the "in crowd," but I was always on the outside looking in! I would like to have been "the queen" of something, but no one ever thought of nominating me. I once heard of a "Possum Queen," and probably would have settled for that! I have no musical talent. I brought home a clarinet and a baritone saxophone, but I didn't get beyond wetting my reed and getting a sore lip. Although I took piano lessons—I wanted to play "Twelfth Street Rag" for Daddy—I never got through Book One. I tried piano lessons even after I was saved and still didn't pass Book One! I thought about taking singing lessons. I could see myself on stage belting out songs as I did my soft-shoe routine. I loved to dance. I would turn on the record player in my bedroom and work up my routines, but they were never seen on stage. My stuffed animals were my only audience. I tried out for the leads in plays. I got parts, but never the lead!

I share all of this, Beloved, to let you see that I tried, but the little I had wasn't enough, until I met Jesus. Then one day as a year-old Christian, I heard Stuart Briscoe say, "God doesn't need your ability. All He needs is your availability!" Availability I had! So I began to make myself available to Him, and in His grace, He took my little bit of faith, which was surrendered to Him, and began to use it.

In John 6, you see quite a contrast between Philip and Andrew, Simon Peter's brother. Philip looked at the hungry multitude from a pragmatic point of view: "There is no way because our natural resources are not adequate enough to pull it off." Andrew, bless his heart, looked to see if there might be a way. He scouted out the situation and came up with a little boy's lunch. "There is a lad here who has five barley loaves and two fish, but what are these for so many people?" (John 6:9).

The loaves were about the size of pancakes, and the fish were fishnet salmon! This lunch wasn't much, in light of the 5000-plus around, and yet it was more than adequate because God was in it.

O Beloved, give Him your small faith, and watch it become more than adequate.

# 39

*J*esus could have been crowned instead of crucified, if He had fulfilled the desire of the people rather than meeting their deeper need. After He fed the multitude they wanted to make Him king because He took care of their temporal needs (John 6:14,15).

But Jesus had a higher purpose. The physical part would die, but the spiritual part of man would live forever. Thus, our Lord needed to go beyond the temporal to the eternal. The sign of the loaves and fish was a springboard for giving the multitude the very precepts of life. Jesus knew the opportunity to teach them would come the next day. And many returned: "So when the crowd saw that Jesus was not there, nor His disciples, they themselves got into the small boats, and came to Capernaum seeking Jesus....[Jesus said,] 'Truly, truly, I say to you, you seek Me, not because you saw signs, but because you ate of the loaves and were filled. Do not work for the food which perishes, but for the food which endures to eternal life, which the Son of Man will give to you, for on Him the Father, God, has set His seal'" (John 6:24,26-27).

Let me ask you a question, Beloved. Why do you follow Jesus? Do you seek Him for the benefits that are yours as a child of God? Because of promises that seem to cover your material needs? Because of some health-wealth doctrine? Because He has healed you? Or because He has taken care of a problem for you?

And what if He didn't meet your temporal needs in a way that you thought He would? What if He allowed you to suffer? What if you asked and didn't receive what you asked for? Would you still embrace Him as your Lord and Savior? Would you still want Him as King of your life? Would you let Him rule if what He was going to ask or expect of you was costly or painful? Have you ever been guilty of seeking Him merely for benefits?

O Beloved, He desires your spiritual good, your eternal good, and that rarely comes in the school of plenty. Rather, it happens usually in the school of discipline or affliction. First the cross and then the crown, for Him and for you.

# 40

$\mathcal{I}$f you seek for signs, then one is not enough to satisfy. You constantly want the reassurance of a miracle. Otherwise, you have to walk in total faith. Miracles and signs are easier, more exciting, concrete "now" evidence. When the multitude asked Jesus, "'What shall we do, so that we may work the works of God?' Jesus answered and said to them, 'This is the work of God, that you believe in Him whom He has sent.' So they said to Him, 'What then do You do for a sign, so that we may see, and believe You? What work do You perform? Our fathers ate the manna in the wilderness; as it is written, "HE GAVE THEM BREAD OUT OF HEAVEN TO EAT"'" (John 6:28-31).

When the multitude reminded Jesus that Moses provided them with daily bread, they weren't considering the fact that there was a day when that bread ceased, a day when God said to Joshua, "Only be strong and very courageous; be careful to do according to all the law which Moses My servant commanded you; do not turn from it to the right or to the left, so that you may have success wherever you go. This book of the law shall not depart from your mouth, but you shall meditate on it day and night, so that you may be careful to do according to all that is written in it…" (Joshua 1:7,8).

In Joshua's day, for the most part, the signs were over. They had seen the power of God; now they were to walk in faith. Now also, with the multitude, it was a matter of believing in the One God had sent down from heaven: Jesus, the true Bread of Life. He was the Bread of God, but they had a hard time understanding that! Jesus reminded them that Moses hadn't given them manna; God had.

The multitudes were missing what God now was giving them "'the true bread out of heaven. For the bread of God is that which comes down out of heaven, and gives life to the world.' Then they said to Him, 'Lord, always give us this bread.' Jesus said to them, 'I am the bread of life; he who comes to Me will not hunger, and he who believes in Me will never thirst. But I said to you that you have seen Me, and yet do not believe'" (John 6:32-36).

It is chilling, isn't it? To think that a person could see Jesus perform His signs, could hear all that He said in His teaching, could talk with Him face-to-face and still not believe in Him. It is heartbreaking to think that people could walk away from the only One who could satisfy a hunger and thirst that came from the very depths of their beings. They walked away because they wanted signs, or a salvation that came by working the works of God. Yet only one thing would do, and that was to believe, to rely on, to trust in Jesus Christ.

O Beloved, we have His Word! We have enough. Read it and believe. "An evil and adulterous generation craves for a sign" (Matthew 12:39). Walk by faith and not by sight. You will be satisfied!

$4$<sub>1</sub>

Before we begin our day together, read John 6:31-71.

Much of what Jesus said was not easy to take! As a matter of fact, after His discourse in the synagogue in Capernaum, many of His disciples said, "This is a difficult statement; who can listen to it?" (John 6:60). What had Jesus said that was difficult to listen to? "As a result of this many of His disciples withdrew and were not walking with Him anymore" (John 6:66). What was it?

Well, Beloved, if you carefully read John 6:31-71, you probably know. This is a passage of Scripture that sometimes brings much controversy and schism in the body of Jesus Christ. How I pray that you will simply let the Word of God say what it says, without trying to take it to extremes that are not warranted in the Word of God.

Many times we become the product of a denomination's particular brand of theology, so that we can't let the Word of God speak for itself. When we view the Word in this way, we often miss what God is saying, because we can't reach a logical conclusion or because we cannot reason it all out in our minds.

We forget that there is a mystery to the gospel. We also forget that we have finite brains compared to the infinite wisdom of God, who says in His Word: "Oh, the depth of the riches both of the wisdom and knowledge of God! How unsearchable are His judgments and unfathomable His ways! For WHO HAS KNOWN THE MIND OF THE LORD,

OR WHO BECAME HIS COUNSELOR? Or WHO HAS FIRST GIVEN TO HIM THAT IT MIGHT BE PAID BACK TO HIM AGAIN? For from Him and through Him and to Him are all things. To Him be the glory forever. Amen" (Romans 11:33-36).

O Beloved, may we never be guilty of putting reason above revelation. When we read difficult sayings, may we not walk away or grumble, as some of Jesus' disciples did, but may we bow the knee in humility and submission and say, "Lord, if it pleases You, it pleases me." "We have believed and have come to know that You are the Holy One of God" (John 6:69).

The statement Jesus made in the synagogue in Capernaum was difficult because He brought those in Galilee face-to-face with the same truth He had given the Jews of Judea: His incarnation. Jesus was the Bread of God who had come down from heaven (John 6:33,58). He was sent by God to do God's will (John 6:38). Therefore, if they did not like what He was doing, they were going against God. Jesus did not act independently from the Father. Thus, when Jesus healed on the Sabbath, it was because God the Father wanted to heal on the Sabbath. The Jews were being confronted with God in the flesh, with One who was telling them that heaven was gained by faith, not works. To the Jew, that was a difficult statement.

# 42

There was more to Jesus' difficult statement than the fact of His incarnation. Jesus also told them, "The bread... which I will give for the life of the world is My flesh" (John 6:51). This statement totally destroyed the illusion that man's works or self-righteousness could ever win eternal life. Whether they believed it or not, they understood His words when He said, "I say to you, unless you eat the flesh of the Son of Man and drink His blood, you have no life in yourselves. He who eats My flesh and drinks My blood has eternal life, and I will raise him up on the last day" (John 6:53,54).

There is only one way to have eternal life, and that is by Jesus abiding in us and we in Him. When Jesus said, "He who eats My flesh and drinks My blood abides in Me, and I in him" (John 6:56), He was showing them the total identification that alone could bring eternal life. There was no other way to heaven. Being a Jew, being circumcised, and keeping the Law wouldn't do it. They had to be united with Him.

All of these things combined to make a difficult statement. But then Jesus made it even harder to take when He put His finger on what kept the Jews from believing. It is interesting that in the period of controversy in Jesus' ministry (John 5 and 6), He did not "tone down" His doctrine. He couldn't because, as He would say later, "My teaching is not Mine, but His who sent Me" (John 7:16).

What was this controversial teaching? It was that God is the initiator of salvation. Listen to what Jesus says:

> All that the Father gives Me will come to Me, and the one who comes to Me I will certainly not cast out (John 6:37).

> This is the will of Him who sent Me, that of all that He has given Me I lose nothing, but raise it up on the last day (John 6:39).

> No one can come to Me unless the Father who sent Me draws him; and I will raise him up on the last day (John 6:44).

> Everyone who has heard and learned from the Father, comes to Me (John 6:45).

> For this reason I have said to you, that no one can come to Me unless it has been granted him from the Father (John 6:65).

What does this show us, Beloved? I believe it shows us our total impotence to save our own souls, and it shows our Father's total sovereignty over life and death! God is God. We do not necessarily know these truths before we are saved. All we may understand is the inscription on the other side of the coin of salvation: "WHOEVER WILL CALL ON THE NAME OF THE LORD WILL BE SAVED" (Romans 10:13). We come to Jesus Christ because we see our sin and His salvation. However, as we get into the Word of God and pore over the Scriptures in childlike faith, we cannot help but see that we came because the Father gave us to the Son. This "difficult saying" prostrates me in wondrous awe and eternal gratitude. How do you feel in light of this incredible truth?

# 43

The fact that God had mercy on you, the fact that He chose you, ought to bring you great comfort and assurance. According to John 6, you came to Jesus because the Father gave you to Him. You came because it was granted to you by the Father. You came because you were drawn by the Father. You came because you heard and learned from the Father (John 6:37,39,44,45,65).

Because the Father is the Author of your salvation, He also will be the Completer of it. Jesus will not cast out those who are given to Him (John 6:37). He does not lose anyone (John 6:39), but raises them up on the last day (John 6:39,40,44,54). "He who began a good work in you [the work of salvation] will perfect it until the day of Christ Jesus" (Philippians 1:6).

This, Beloved, is your blessed assurance. It is not license to sin, to walk your own way, to deny Jesus and live your own life. Those who are true children of God will manifest the reality of their salvation by their continuance in the faith (Hebrews 3:6,14; 1 John 2:19; Colossians 1:23; 1 Corinthians 15:2). Judas is an example of those who look like believers but aren't.

When some of the disciples walked away because of Jesus' teaching, "Jesus said to the twelve, 'You do not want to go away also, do you?' Simon Peter answered Him, 'Lord, to whom shall we go? You have words of eternal life. We have believed and have come to know that You are the Holy One of God'" (John 6:67-69).

After Jesus talked about those who were His being given by the Father to the Son and after He explained they would not be cast out but would be raised up on the last day, He also let the twelve know that Judas' actions would not negate these truths. Thus, when Peter, as the spokesman of the group, avowed the fact that they had truly believed in Jesus, "Jesus answered them, 'Did I Myself not choose you, the twelve, and yet one of you is a devil?' Now He meant Judas the son of Simon Iscariot, for he, one of the twelve, was going to betray Him" (John 6:70,71).

It is interesting, isn't it, that right up until they celebrated the last Passover together, just before Jesus' arrest, none of the disciples could tell that Judas was the one ("a devil," Jesus called him)? It wasn't that Judas lost his salvation; it was that he never was saved. The Father never gave Judas to the Son. But at the same time, let me assure you that Judas made his choice. It isn't that he wanted to be saved but couldn't be. Judas had every opportunity that the other apostles had, but he never, so to speak, ate Jesus' flesh and drank His blood. He never had eternal life.

But you may say to me, "It doesn't fit. How could both statements be true? If God didn't give Judas to Jesus, doesn't that leave Judas with no choice?" No, Beloved. Leave it alone. This is a revelation you don't try to reason out. You simply bow the knee and believe what God says. Judas betrayed Jesus. He acted by choice and regretted it, but he never repented.

Thank God today for His mercy. Thank Him that He is giving you opportunities to respond.

# 44

Therefore many other signs Jesus also performed in the presence of the disciples, which are not written in this book; but these have been written so that you may believe that Jesus is the Christ, the Son of God; and that believing you may have life in His name" (John 20:30,31). Three other Gospels had been written, and yet a fourth was necessary. A Gospel was needed that would show, without a shadow of a doubt, that Jesus was the Christ, the Messiah, the One promised in the Old Testament. A Gospel was needed to focus on the central fact that Jesus is God.

Let us never forget to keep the purpose of the Gospel of John before us, for it is the key to proper understanding and interpretation. The first 11 chapters of John lay before us a selected number of signs performed by Jesus which conclusively prove that Jesus was the Son of God, God in the flesh. The whole thrust of this Gospel is the deity of Jesus Christ. You know that when one refers to the deity of Christ it is another way of saying that Jesus is God. It calls us to understand that He possesses the same character, the same attributes as God the Father, although they are two separate Persons.

The relationship of Jesus Christ to God is that of Sonship. Jesus is the only begotten Son of God. As the Son of God, He holds a unique position. We become sons of God by virtue of the new birth. We are "born not of blood nor of the will of the flesh nor of the will of man, but of God" (John 1:13). Jesus was not born; He was not created. He has always existed: "In the beginning was the Word, and the Word was with God, and the Word was God. He was in the beginning with God.... And the Word became flesh, and dwelt among us, and we saw His glory, glory as of the only begotten from the Father, full of grace and truth" (John 1:1,2,14).

Jesus became man, God in the flesh, through the virgin birth. God placed Jesus in the womb of the virgin Mary so that He might take upon Himself flesh and blood. "Therefore, since the children share in flesh and blood, He Himself likewise also partook of the same, that through death He might render powerless him who had the power of death, that is, the devil" (Hebrews 2:14).

Man's sin gave Satan the power of death over man, for sin puts man under the power of Satan (Ephesians 2:1-3). Therefore, when "God so loved the world, that He gave His only begotten Son, that whoever believes in Him shall not perish, but have eternal life" (John 3:16), God enabled us to be set free from sin. Therefore, the very minute we believe in the Lord Jesus Christ, God removes us from Satan's power of death by making us His children.

When we believe in the Lord Jesus Christ, we pass "out of death into life" (John 5:24). We are turned from darkness into light, from the power of Satan into the kingdom of God, where we receive forgiveness of sins and an inheritance among those who are sanctified (Acts 26:18).

Thank God today that Jesus is the Son of God! Thank Him that Jesus became the Son of Man to render powerless him who had the power of death, so that you might have life!

# 45

$\mathcal{A}$s you read through the Gospel of John, you see that Jesus constantly demonstrated the life that would belong to those who believe. In John 3, we see that life which comes in His name begins with the new birth (3:3-5). In John 4, we see that it is a life that quenches our thirst, satisfying that unexplained craving within the soul of every person for eternal life (4:10,14). In John 5, we see that it is a life that is to be lived in total dependence upon the Father as shown to us in the relationship of the Son to the Father (5:19,30). In John 6, we see that it is a life of total identity with the Son as we abide in Him and He in us (6:56).

Now as we turn to John 7, we are going to see that it is a life which will be lived on a different timetable, a different dimension than that of the world. This life in a different dimension will put us into conflict with the world. And yet, as Jesus says, "If the world hates you, you know that it has hated Me before it hated you. If you were of the world, the world would love its own; but because you are not of the world, but I chose you out of the world, because of this the world hates you. Remember the word that I said to you, 'A slave is not greater than his master.' If they persecuted Me, they will also persecute you; if they kept My word, they will keep yours also. But all these things they will do to you for My name's sake, because they do not know the One who sent Me" (John 15:18-21).

As John 7 opens, we find Jesus in conflict with His half brothers because they are "of the world." They do not understand that Jesus is not of this world, that He has a different Father. They can't comprehend that He doesn't operate on the same level of worldly reasoning. He lives life on a different timetable, from an eternal perspective.

It was the Feast of Tabernacles, the fall of the year, the month of Tishri when every Jew was to go to Jerusalem to celebrate the feast and live in booths made from branches of trees. "Therefore His brothers said to Him, 'Leave here and go into Judea, so that Your disciples also may see Your works which You are doing. For no one does anything in secret when he himself seeks to be known publicly. If You do these things, show Yourself to the world.' For not even His brothers were believing in Him. So Jesus said to them, 'My time is not yet here, but your time is always opportune. The world cannot hate you, but it hates Me because I testify of it, that its deeds are evil'" (John 7:3-7).

O Beloved, are there members of your family who do not understand you because, like Jesus' brothers, they have not believed on Him? Is there a conflict because they do not understand your lifestyle? Because they want to tell you how you should spend your time and what you should give yourself to? Jesus understands. Talk to Him about it.

# 46

We are so conscious of time. To some, time drags. To others, time is fleeting. To the Christian, time is precious. Yet, we are never to live under its pressure. Like our Lord, we are to live on God's timetable, for it is to God that we shall be accountable for how we spend our time.

How I have had to learn this! There are so many demands on my time because of the type of ministry to which the Lord has called me. I have had to learn to say no. Sometimes that is very difficult because I feel people may not understand. Then I go back to Scriptures like John 7 and am comforted and reassured by the life of my Lord.

In the body of Christ, it seems that many have so little time for the Word of God and the work of ministry because they have entangled themselves "in the affairs of everyday life" (2 Timothy 2:4). In Ephesians 5:15,16 we read: "Therefore be careful [literally, look carefully] how you walk, not as unwise men but as wise, making the most of your time, because the days are evil."

We are to redeem the time, as the King James Version says, to make the most of our time. There are two other principles we need to remember also. *Our times are in His hand.* Psalm 31:13-15 says, "For I have heard the slander of many, terror is on every side; while they took counsel together against me, they schemed to take away my life. But as for me, I trust in You, O LORD, I say, 'You are my God.' My times are in Your hand; deliver me from the hand of my enemies and from those who persecute me."

This is a principle our Lord certainly had to live by, because the Jews were constantly trying to take His life. John 7 opens with this statement: "After these things Jesus was walking in Galilee; for He was unwilling to walk in Judea because the Jews were seeking to kill Him." Yet later, we find Jesus going to Judea during the Feast of Tabernacles. Although His life is being threatened, He can go in confidence because He knows that His times are also in God's hand. Thus, we read: "They were seeking to seize Him; and no man laid his hand on Him, because His hour had not yet come" (John 7:30). "His hour had not yet come" is a reference to the time of His crucifixion, a time set by the Father.

The second principle is that *our days are numbered by God.* Psalm 139:16 says, "Your eyes have seen my unformed substance; and in Your book were all written the days that were ordained for me, when as yet there was not one of them." No need to be ruled by the fear of death or the pressure of man, Beloved. We move on a different timetable— God's.

# 47

*T*here are two truths I want to share so you can live in such a way so as not to be ashamed when you see your heavenly Father face-to-face.

The first truth, which I mentioned yesterday, is that you are to *daily redeem the time,* to make the most of it. God has numbered your days. Although you do not know your length of days, you are still to live in the light of the fact that they could end at any time. When your days end, there will be no more time to live for God, to walk in the good works He has foreordained for you to walk in (Ephesians 2:10). When you redeem the time, you commit each day to the lordship of Jesus Christ and walk in faith's obedience. Then whenever your days come to an end, you will not be ashamed.

I believe that is how it was with Sallie Irby, one of our Precept coordinators and trainers. Single and 37, Sallie was a dynamic woman of God whose life packed a spiritual wallop, impacting the lives of so many. She had just told her friend and co-laborer, Julie, that she felt God was getting ready to do something special in her life. It *was* special! She got to see her Father God in person. About a week later, Sallie was killed in an accident. Days before her death, Sallie sat with Julie and me in the lobby of our Administration Building, talking of the future of Precept Bible studies in her area. Sallie was redeeming the time!

The second truth you need to remember is that *God is sovereign.* He is in control of all of time, all of history. He "does according to His will in the host of heaven and among the inhabitants of earth; and no one can ward off His hand or say to Him, 'What have You done?'" (Daniel 4:35). Therefore, God is never caught off guard. God does not make snap decisions, nor is He suddenly confronted with a problem He has not foreseen. "For the LORD of hosts has planned, and who can frustrate it?" (Isaiah 14:27). Your sovereign God is in control of all your problems, as well as your solutions. "Besides Me there is no God....I am the LORD, and there is no other, the One forming light and creating darkness, causing well-being and creating calamity; I am the LORD who does all these" (Isaiah 45:5-7).

Sallie's death was under God's sovereignty. God's purpose *will not* be thwarted. Therefore, Beloved, you can move according to His timetable. Be in tune to God. Redeem your days, being careful how you spend your time. Then in His sovereignty, when He calls you home, you, like Sallie, will be able to say, "I glorified You on the earth, having accomplished the work which You have given Me to do" (John 17:4).

# 48

$\mathcal{A}$s you read through the Gospel of John, you are acutely aware that our Lord was in the world but not of it. He was on earth, but He lived life on a higher plane. You see His life, and you long to live like He did. And you know what, Beloved? It is possible, for Jesus lived as God intends us to live, as God has provided for us to live. As the Son of Man, Jesus lived His life in total dependence upon the Father. And, Beloved, you and I can live that way too by the Spirit.

I would like you to read through John 7 from the perspective of living life in a different dimension. If you are going to live in this other dimension, then there will be no self-promotion. As you read John 7:1-9, you see Jesus' brothers urging Him to promote Himself, to make the most of the world's opportunities. They felt the Feast of Tabernacles would be a good time for Him to work His miracles in Jerusalem. If Jesus wanted to be known publicly, then He needed to show Himself to the world!

If you are going to live in God's dimension and not the world's, you must live on the basis of His teaching, His Word, not your own pet theories, philosophy, psychology, traditions, or prejudiced interpretations. In John 7:14-18, Jesus tells us that His teaching was not His. Rather it was "His who sent Me" (verse 16). "He who speaks from himself seeks his own glory" (verse 18).

How careful we must be in handling the precepts of God, that we do not read or interpret the Word through our prejudices. This is a matter of the will. Jesus says, "If anyone is willing to do His will, he will know of the teaching, whether it is of God or whether I speak from Myself" (John 7:17). If we are willing to do God's will, then we should have discernment in evaluating what we hear that is supposedly from the Word of God. In his *Word Studies,* Marvin Vincent says, "Sympathy with the will of God is a condition of understanding it."[6] The Pharisees lived on tradition, placing it above the Word. Life in a different dimension is based on everything that proceeds out of the mouth of God (Deuteronomy 8:3).

What place does the Word of God have in your life? How willing are you to do His will as revealed in His Word?

# 49

Things are not always as they seem. Therefore, if we are going to live in a different dimension, we must not judge according to appearance. In John 7:19-24, we find the Jews bent on killing Jesus. Their plot was not known by the multitude; however, it is obvious that most of the people were not sympathetic toward our Lord.

Like the Jews, the multitudes were not judging with righteous judgment but according to appearance. They were running on emotion, caught up in the heat of the moment. They were running on a "mob mentality." They were blindly following their leaders without responsibly evaluating the situation. They were going strictly by the way things seemed. They had not stopped to think things through, to seek the wisdom of God.

Thus, while Jesus was teaching in the Temple, He exposed the treachery of the Jews' hearts: "Did not Moses give you the Law, and yet none of you carries out the Law? Why do you seek to kill Me?" (John 7:19). The Jews had missed the reality that the Law went deeper than external obedience. This is so well explained in the Sermon on the Mount when Jesus told His disciples, "For I say to you that unless your righteousness surpasses that of the scribes and Pharisees, you will not enter the kingdom of heaven" (Matthew 5:20). The scribes and Pharisees had an external righteousness, but that was all. They held to the letter of the Law, but they missed the heart of the Law. Thus, in the Sermon on the Mount, our Lord explains an inward righteousness, which would see its outworking in obedience to the Law of God.

Although the Jews would justify their plot to put Jesus to death by accusing Him of breaking some aspect of the Law which was punishable by death, still what they intentionally planned to do was kill Him. This plan was nothing short of murder!

Have you ever had anger in your heart toward another because you judged according to appearance rather than with righteous judgment?

# 50

$D$o not judge according to appearance, but judge with righteous judgment" (John 7:24) was Jesus' statement to the multitude. He exposed the Jews' plot to kill Him when He said, "Did not Moses give you the Law, and yet none of you carries out the Law? Why do you seek to kill Me?" (John 7:19). Here was the only One who would ever perfectly fulfill the Law, and yet they were accusing Him of breaking the Law because He had healed a man on the Sabbath. And the whole time they had murder in their hearts! Then when Jesus exposed their desire to kill Him, "the crowd answered, 'You have a demon! Who seeks to kill You?'" (John 7:20).

Beloved, can you see the blindness of those who judge by appearance and not by righteous judgment, who get hot over an issue and spiel off before they evaluate the situation? Do you suppose there were those in this crowd who would later join the mob shouting, "Not this Man, but Barabbas," when they could have chosen Jesus? Men who would shout, "Crucify Him!" as they became pawns in the Jews' desire to exterminate Jesus? Here He was, God incarnate, and they were accusing Him of having a demon!

Have you ever had anyone judge you unjustly? Has anyone ever accused you of being on the side of Satan when you were standing for God?

I have received letters from people who have judged me because of my clothing or because I wore earrings, a wedding band, a ring, and a necklace. Their questions have made me careful to examine what I wear. But what hurt me was their accusations against my heart, all because they did not approve of my appearance. I constantly seek to be pure before God. They judged me according to appearance.

But do you know the result of such instances in my own life? I have realized that I have been guilty of the same thing toward others. I have been brought up short! I need to give others what I want for myself—judgment that is not according to appearance but according to righteous judgment.

How can we do this? First, never judge according to the letter of the Law. Always look at the heart of the Law. For instance, the Sabbath was for man's benefit. Therefore, if one could circumcise on the Sabbath, why couldn't a man be healed on the Sabbath (John 7:22,23)?

Second, don't accuse; find out the facts. Get the "victim's" side of the story. Third, let him explain his heart. What happened may have been a distortion of what was in his heart. If he says it was, then give him the benefit of the doubt. Fourth, walk in love. Love hopes, believes, and endures all things.

Determine before the Father to judge as you'd like to be judged.

## 5

*A*re you a people-pleaser? Because I've always wanted to be liked, I need to be very careful in this area. I have not always won the war! But since God knows my heart, since He knows I want to live in a different dimension, He is always faithful to show me when I have failed.

If we are going to live life on a higher plane, we must not be pleasers of men, but of God. I teach teenagers as well as adults, and this has been a joy to my heart. Each year we have Teen Conferences and an annual Summer Boot Camp for teens at Precept Ministries headquarters. These times are designed to equip the teens as soldiers for the Lord.

I often ask the teens questions to keep me in touch and current with where they are coming from. I ask them to answer anonymously. To the question, "What is the greatest pressure you face?" the number-one answer is "peer pressure." They feel pressured to conform to the crowd!

You can see why a strong family bond is so important. When a child receives security and acceptance at home, he doesn't feel driven to seek it someplace else.

Teens aren't the only ones who have to deal with pressures to conform. Adults are constantly confronted with the pressures of a world that says you have to conform if you are going to make it. This is why our relationship with our heavenly Parent is so important. The stronger the relationship, the greater our resistance to conform to the world, to please men rather than God. And like the teens I mentioned, the more we are sure of the Father's total acceptance, the freer we are from needing acceptance from the world.

As you read John 7, you can see that the crowds were being greatly influenced by the Jews. The fear of men was bringing a snare. In fact, it was keeping some from believing on the only One who could ever satisfy their deepest needs. In John 7:13 we read: "Yet no one was speaking openly of Him for fear of the Jews." What a contrast this is with our Lord who said, "And He who sent Me is with Me; He has not left Me alone, for I always do the things that are pleasing to Him" (John 8:29).

If you are going to live in a different dimension, you should constantly ask yourself, "Am I now seeking the favor of men, or of God? Or am I striving to please men? If I were still trying to please men, I would not be a bond-servant of Christ" (Galatians 1:10).

## 52

$\mathcal{T}$he key to living life in a different dimension is life in the Spirit. Jesus knew He was teaching a mixed multitude, people who were following Him for all sorts of reasons. As they sought Him at the feast, they asked, " 'Where is He?' There was much grumbling among the crowds concerning Him; some were saying, 'He is a good man'; others were saying, 'No, on the contrary, He leads the people astray' " (John 7:11,12).

Yet among them were those who had a genuine thirst for life on a different dimension. So, "on the last day, the great day of the feast, Jesus stood and cried out, saying, 'If anyone is thirsty, let him come to Me and drink. He who believes in Me, as the Scripture said, "From his innermost being will flow rivers of living water." ' But this He spoke of the Spirit, whom those who believed in Him were to receive; for the Spirit was not yet given, because Jesus was not yet glorified" (John 7:37-39).

What a proclamation that was! The Spirit of God indwelling any who thirsted? Under the Old Covenant, the Spirit of God came intermittently upon priests, prophets, and kings. Here was the New Covenant promise of the Spirit being given to anyone who thirsted, who believed in Jesus. And it would be such an indwelling that rivers of living water would flow from a person's innermost being continuously!

From the days of Moses and Leviticus, the Jews had added a great deal of ceremony to the Feast of Booths. Every day except the last day, the priests would go to the pool of Siloam and fill their pitchers with water. Then they would return to the Temple area and with the blast of trumpets would march seven times around the altar and then pour water from the pitchers, while they sang Isaiah 12:3: "Therefore with joy shall ye draw water out of the wells of salvation" (KJV). They would sing the Hallel, Psalms 113 through 118, ending with:

> The stone which the builders rejected has become the chief corner stone. This is the LORD's doing; it is marvelous in our eyes. This is the day which the LORD has made; let us rejoice and be glad in it. O LORD, do save, we beseech You; O LORD, we beseech You, do send prosperity! Blessed is the one who comes in the name of the LORD; we have blessed you from the house of the LORD. The LORD is God, and He has given us light; bind the festival sacrifice with cords to the horns of the altar. You are my God, and I give thanks to You; You are my God, I extol You. Give thanks to the LORD, for He is good; for His lovingkindness is everlasting (Psalm 118:22-29).

The One about whom they sang was in their presence! He was the stone the builders would reject. But to others, He became the foundation stone for life in a different dimension, life in the Spirit.

## 5

You can't live in a different dimension—above the pull of the flesh, the pressures of people, the philosophies of the world—unless you live and walk by the indwelling Spirit of God. Life in this dimension is one of continuous dependence, continuous abiding. To put it in the words of John 7, this life is a continual coming and drinking. In John 7:37 Jesus says, "If anyone is thirsty, let him come to Me and drink." The literal meaning of the words is, "Let him keep coming to Me, and let him keep drinking."

O what a Hallel they sang when Jesus stood and cried out this promise on that last day of the feast! Day by day they had poured out water from their golden pitchers on the altar, and now the Water of Life was among them. It was from God's altar, the cross, that the indwelling of the Spirit would be made possible. For not until Christ was glorified in His death, burial, resurrection, and ascension could the blessed Holy Spirit come to indwell man and be the pledge of our inheritance of eternal life (Ephesians 1:14).

The priests had sung, "Blessed is the one who comes in the name of the LORD" (Psalm 118:26), and there He was! But were they blessing Him? No! For the most part, the religious leaders were seeking to get rid of Him.

They recited, "Bind the festival sacrifice with cords to the horns of the altar." But they missed the fact that the Lamb of God who would take away the sin of the world was standing in their midst. During the Feast of Tabernacles, the Jews would light four huge candelabra called *menorahs*. Jesus, the Light of the World, stood before them as they sang, "The LORD is God, and He has given us light" (Psalm 118:27). Remember how John opens his Gospel? "In Him was life, and the life was the Light of men. The Light shines in the darkness, and the darkness did not comprehend it.…There was the true Light which, coming into the world, enlightens every man" (1:4,5,9).

Again and again Jesus referred to Himself as "the Light of the world," and promised that those who follow Him will not walk in darkness (John 8:12). Again, Beloved, you have it—life on a different timetable because it is life in the Spirit.

O Beloved, have you drunk of the Fountain of living waters? If you have, the Spirit within has witnessed with your spirit that you are a child of God. Then, "walk by the Spirit, and you will not carry out the desire of the flesh" (Galatians 5:16). You will live life on the highest plane.

# What Does it Mean to Truly Believe Jesus Is the Christ

JOHN 8

## 54

To be born in sin is something we cannot help, for "in sin my mother conceived me" (Psalm 51:5). We are all sinners at birth, bearing the consequence of Adam and Eve's sin in the Garden of Eden, for "through one man sin entered into the world, and death through sin" (Romans 5:12).

However, no human being has to die in his sin. Remember, the Gospel of John was written that "you may believe that Jesus is the Christ, the Son of God; and that believing you may have life in His name" (John 20:31). Believing that Jesus is God causes us to pass from death to life, from the kingdom of Satan to the kingdom of heaven.

What does it truly mean to "believe that Jesus is the Christ, the Son of God"? It means believing that Jesus Christ is God in the flesh, one with the Father in nature. Or to put it another way, it is to believe in the deity of Jesus Christ.

When we speak of the deity of Jesus, we mean Jesus is God. According to the Word of God, if you do not believe in the deity of Jesus Christ, you will "die in your sins" (John 8:24).

To "die in your sins" means that you will spend eternity in the lake of fire where the worm dies not and the fire is not quenched (Mark 9:43-48). To "die in your sins" is to miss heaven! To miss life!

For the next several days, I want us to look at the deity of Jesus Christ. Because this doctrine distinguishes true Christianity from the cults, it is crucial that we understand it. I want you to be able to "contend earnestly for the faith which was once for all handed down to the saints" (Jude 3). Therefore, let me give you an outline which we will follow. Day by day, we will cover these points: Jesus Christ is God because: 1) He is eternal; 2) He is the Word, explaining the Father—a) as the radiance of His glory, b) as the exact representation of His nature, c) as the "I AM," d) as being one with the Father, e) as possessor of the sovereign rights of God; 3) He is Creator; 4) in Him is life; and 5) He is Lord.

Study well and ask God the Father to reveal truth upon truth to you as we turn to behold the deity of the Lord Jesus Christ.

# 55

*Jesus Christ is God because He is eternal.* He has always been; He will always be. In the very first words of his Gospel, John sets out to establish unequivocally that Jesus is the promised Messiah, the Son of God. John accomplishes this by showing that Jesus, like the Father, is eternal: "In the beginning was the Word, and the Word was with God, and the Word was God. He was in the beginning with God" (John 1:1,2). Then so there is no doubt as to who "the Word" is, John says further, "And the Word became flesh, and dwelt among us, and we saw His glory, glory as of the only begotten from the Father, full of grace and truth" (1:14).

When John tells us under the inspiration of the Holy Spirit that the Word is "the only begotten from the Father," it does not mean that Jesus was created by God or had a beginning in time. No, Beloved, when it says that Jesus is "the only begotten from the Father," it is referring to His incarnation when mankind would behold His glory as of the *only* begotten *from* the Father. We must never forget that there is only one Man in all of time who was uniquely God and Man—the Lord Jesus Christ.

It is vital that you understand this truth, Beloved, for there are some who teach that we are God. Yes, God *indwells* the person who believes on the Lord Jesus Christ, but that person will never *become* God. That is heresy!

O Beloved, beware of anyone who teaches this damnable doctrine, for it is straight from the devil who wanted to be as God and who persuaded Eve that she could be as God through disobedience to the clear command of God. How I pray that God will use this devotional study to establish you in His Word, so you won't be carried about by every wind of doctrine and cunning craftiness of men by which they lie in wait to deceive you (Ephesians 4:13,14).

Remember that Jesus alone is God. He is the Eternal One. Micah 5:2 prophesied His birth and, at the same time, showed us His eternity: "But as for you, Bethlehem Ephrathah, too little to be among the clans of Judah, from you One will go forth for Me to be ruler in Israel. His goings forth are from long ago, from the days of eternity." Jesus has always been and will always be uniquely the Son of God who became the Son of Man.

# 56

*Jesus Christ is God because He is the Word, and as the Lord, He explains the Father.* Many have said to me that they can relate to Jesus Christ, but they have a hard time relating to God the Father. This is either because they have a distorted image of a father, or because they cannot understand the actions of God in the Old Testament. Usually, it is because of earthly fathers who were distant, harsh, uncaring, absent, unreasonably demanding, cruel, or perverted. Therefore, it is easy to understand why they have a hard time in developing an intimate relationship with God.

However, Jesus came to remove that distance. "No one has seen God at any time; the only begotten God who is in the bosom of the Father, He has explained Him" (John 1:18). Your image of God the Father may have been distorted by an earthly father. However, this distortion can be corrected if you will get to know Jesus Christ. You must believe and embrace the truth of the Word of God above your feelings.

Jesus has explained your heavenly Father. As you embrace truth and walk in it, and as you continue to spend time in the Word, you will come to know the true character of your heavenly Father, and will become more secure and comfortable in His unconditional love. Jesus is the Word become flesh, so that you might know God, and that God might become your Father through His Son. And who is the Son? He is God.

Let's go back to John 1:18 for a moment. Remember our subject is the deity of Jesus Christ, understanding and embracing the truth of it so that you do not die in your sins. In John 1:18, we see Jesus as "the only begotten God who is in the bosom of the Father." Once again, John uses the phrase, "the only begotten" as he did in John 1:14. Remember, *begotten* does not refer to the creation of Jesus, for He has always been. Jesus is eternal. He has no beginning; He has no end. He has always existed; He will always exist. He is God—one with the Father and yet separate as a Person.

If you ever say the Nicene Creed, you remember the phrase referring to Jesus which says "begotten, not made." The fathers of the faith wanted to make sure that Christians understand that Jesus is not a created being. Rather He is God, equal with the Father in His eternal existence.

He was begotten as the Son of Man: "Since the children share in flesh and blood, He Himself likewise also partook of the same, that through death He might render powerless him who had the power of death, that is, the devil" (Hebrews 2:14). Therefore, it was planned in the eternal counsels of God that "by the grace of God He might taste death for everyone" (Hebrews 2:9).

Who was it who hung upon Calvary's cross? It was the only begotten God, God the Son, explaining the unconditional love of God the Father.

# 57

*J*esus can explain the Father to us because He has always been with God. *He can also explain the Father to us because He is the radiance of His glory.*

The basis, or should I say the "seedbed" of doctrinal truth regarding the deity of Jesus Christ as taught in the Gospel of John, is found in the first verses of his Gospel: "In the beginning was the Word, and the Word was with God, and the Word was God. He was in the beginning with God. All things came into being through Him, and apart from Him nothing came into being that has come into being. In Him was life, and the life was the Light of men" (1:1-4).

Before you go any further, Beloved, I want you to stop and list in your notebook everything that you learn about the Word from John 1:1-4. John tells us, without a shadow of doubt, that the Word is Jesus who became flesh and dwelt among us, showing us His glory, the glory of the Father.

Hebrews 1 is another key chapter of the Bible that stresses the deity of Jesus Christ. "[God] in these last days has spoken to us in His Son....And He is the radiance of His glory" (Hebrews 1:2-3). The Greek word for *glory* is *doxa,* which comes from *dokeō,* meaning "to seem." Therefore, *glory* refers to the nature and the acts of God in His self-manifestation. To glorify someone means to give a high estimate of who they are to others. If you see Jesus, you see the Father, for Jesus is the radiance of His glory. Ponder this truth in your heart.

# 58

*H*ave you beheld the glory of Jesus, Beloved? Have you seen that He truly is the radiance of God's glory? Throughout the Gospel of John, the words *glory* and *glorify* are used repeatedly, for John's purpose in writing is that you might believe that Jesus is the Christ, the Son of God, and one with the Father. To see Jesus is to see the Father, for Jesus is the radiant light of God's glory. Hallelujah!

Don't miss the awesome statement John makes in 12:41. Having quoted Isaiah 53:1 and Isaiah 6:10, John says, "These things Isaiah said because he saw His glory, and he spoke of Him." The words *His glory* and *Him* are references to Jesus Christ. Note in the following verses how the pronouns refer back to Jesus: "These things Jesus spoke, and He went away and hid Himself from them. But though He had performed so many signs before them, yet they were not believing in Him. This was to fulfill the word of Isaiah the prophet which he spoke, 'LORD, WHO HAS BELIEVED OUR REPORT? AND TO WHOM HAS THE ARM OF THE LORD BEEN REVEALED?' For this reason they could not believe, for Isaiah said again, 'HE HAS BLINDED THEIR EYES AND HE HARDENED THEIR HEART, SO THAT THEY WOULD NOT SEE WITH THEIR EYES AND PERCEIVE WITH THEIR HEART, AND BE CONVERTED AND I HEAL THEM.' These things Isaiah said because he saw His glory, and he spoke of Him" (John 12:36-41).

Isaiah 6 and 53 are prophecies of Jesus in His preincarnate state. Isaiah shows us the deity of Jesus Christ as the radiance of God's glory.

No other Old Testament prophet gives us a greater description of our Lord Jesus Christ.

In Isaiah 6:1-3, he tells us of seeing the Lord on His throne, "lofty and exalted," with the seraphim calling out, "Holy, Holy, Holy, is the LORD of hosts, the whole earth is full of His glory." Then we read of Isaiah's conviction of his sin and the purging of that sin so that his iniquity is taken away and his sin is forgiven. After this, Isaiah writes, "Then I heard the voice of the Lord, saying, 'Whom shall I send, and who will go for Us?'" (6:8).

Whoa! Did you note "Who will go for *Us?*" The "Us" implies more than one. The "Us," beloved reader, shows that more than God the Father is there. The Son is there, and we are seeing His glory, for He is one with the Father—one in nature, one in attributes, one in glory.

## 59

*T*he glory emanating from the Son is the radiant light of God's glory. To see Jesus is to see the Father, for They are one in nature. As John 1:1 says, "The Word was with God." From the very beginning, Jesus was completely identified with the Father. Throughout his Gospel, John confirms this truth, for he knows that if we do not believe that Jesus is God, we will surely perish.

In Jesus' high priestly prayer, He makes this statement: "Now, Father, glorify Me together with Yourself, with the glory which I had with You before the world was" (John 17:5). Glory belongs to God alone. "I am the LORD, that is My name; I will not give My glory to another" (Isaiah 42:8). God will not share His glory with man.

Jesus is the One of whom Isaiah wrote: "For a child will be born to us, a son will be given to us; and the government will rest on His shoulders; and His name will be called Wonderful Counselor, Mighty God, Eternal Father, Prince of Peace" (9:6). Jesus was born as a child, but given as a son! Because Jesus has always been the Son of God, when He came to earth as God's Son, He was given to us. However, He was born as the incarnate Son of Man.

Jesus became a man, taking on, as Philippians 2:7 says, "the likeness of men." In all the Word of God, there is no greater passage on the incarnation than Philippians 2. Yet in the same passage, we once again have confirmed to us the deity of Jesus Christ: "Have this attitude in yourselves which was also in Christ Jesus, who, although He existed in the form of God, did not regard equality with God a thing to be grasped, but emptied Himself, taking the form of a bond-servant, and being made in the likeness of men. Being found in appearance as a man, He humbled Himself by becoming obedient to the point of death, even death on a cross" (Philippians 2:5-8).

Jesus became the Son of Man, and for the rest of eternity He will bear man's likeness, having regained for man what was lost by Adam. Because the Son of God was born a man, because He paid sin's penalty as a man, because He was raised from the dead as a man, you and I who believe these truths so as to submit to Him as God will sit with Him, ruling and reigning forever (Revelation 1:6; 2:26,27; 5:9,10).

# 60

*O* Beloved, where do you run when you are confused? Where do you run when you are without strength? Where do you run when you still need the arms and security of a father? Where do you run when turmoil rages within or without?

You can run to Jesus! His name is "Wonderful Counselor." He will instruct you in the way you should go (Psalm 32:8). His name is "Mighty God." You can exchange your strength for His. His name is "Eternal Father." He has loved you with an everlasting love (Jeremiah 31:3). He has engraved you on the palms of His hands (Isaiah 49:16). He will never leave you nor forsake you (Hebrews 13:5). As a father pities his children, so He pities you (Psalm 103:13). He is "Prince of Peace," so "do not let your heart be troubled" (John 14:1). In the world, you shall have tribulation. But take courage, Jesus has overcome the world (John 16:33). And this is the victory that has overcome the world—your faith (1 John 5:4).

"Cursed is the man who trusts in mankind and makes flesh his strength, and whose heart turns away from the LORD." But, "blessed is the man who trusts in the LORD and whose trust is the LORD" (Jeremiah 17:5,7). You can run to Him because He is God.

Not only is Jesus the radiance of God's glory, but *He is also the Word, explaining the Father as the exact representation of God's nature* (Hebrews 1:3). When we speak of the nature of God, we are referring to the very essence of God, those attributes which make God uniquely God. The word *representation* in Hebrews 1:3 is from the Greek *charaktēr*. A *charaktēr* was the impress made by a die or seal. It gave the idea of exact correspondence to the object whose image it bore.

When I was in my early teens, it became the fad to use sealing wax on our letters. We would buy a stick of wax in our favorite color and then melt it over the flap of the envelope. Then while the wax was still warm and soft, we would make an impression of the letters of our name or of a signet ring. This left the impress of our "symbol."

You may think that the phrases "radiance of His glory" and "exact representation of His nature" mean the same thing. However, there is a difference that is beautiful in its contrast. In the phrase "radiance of His glory," we see Jesus' total identity with the Father. In the phrase "exact representation of His nature," we see that Jesus and the Father are two distinct Beings possessing the same character, the same attributes.

Jesus is all that God is. He does not just have what God has. There is a difference!

# 61

$\mathcal{J}$esus does not merely possess some of what God has. He *is* all that God is! He is equal with the Father, possessing every attribute of God. He is not merely One in whom the Father dwells, in the way that He indwells every born-again child of God through the Holy Spirit. Jesus is the very essence of God "the exact representation of His nature" (Hebrews 1:3). The same truth is seen in the Gospel of John in the statement that "the Word was with God" (1:1).

In the phrase "the Word *was* God," we see a parallel to the phrase "He is the radiance of His glory" from Hebrews 1:3. In the phrase "the Word was *with* God," we see the parallel in Hebrews 1:3 to "the exact representation of His nature." The latter shows Jesus as a distinct Person apart from the Father and yet possessing the same nature as God.

In John 14:6, Jesus has just told the 11 apostles that He is the way to the Father when Philip says, "Lord, show us the Father, and it is enough for us." To which Jesus replies, "Have I been so long with you, and yet you have not come to know Me, Philip? He who has seen Me has seen the Father; how can you say, 'Show us the Father'? Do you not believe that I am in the Father, and the Father is in Me?" (14:8-10).

To see Jesus was to see God because Jesus is the exact representation of His nature. Paul brings this out so powerfully in Colossians 1:15-17 when, speaking of Jesus, he writes: "He is the image of the invisible God, the firstborn of all creation. For by Him all things were created, both in the heavens and on earth, visible and invisible, whether thrones or dominions or rulers or authorities—all things have been created through Him and for Him. He is before all things, and in Him all things hold together."

Some who do not believe in the deity and incarnation of Jesus Christ such as the Mormons, Jehovah's Witnesses, or those involved in Christian Science or the Way International like to point you to Colossians 1:15: "the firstborn of all creation." They use this phrase to say that Jesus was created by God, that He is not eternal but had a beginning.

However, to make it say this goes against the context of this passage and also against the context of all of Scripture, for as we have seen, Jesus is eternal. "Firstborn of all creation" refers to priority of position. Paul's point in this passage is to show that Jesus rightfully has "first place" or preeminence "in everything" because He is God (Colossians 1:18). All was created through Him and for Him—even you, Beloved!

# 62

He is also head of the body, the church; and He is the beginning, the firstborn from the dead, so that He Himself will come to have first place in everything. For it was the Father's good pleasure for all the fullness to dwell in Him, and through Him to reconcile all things to Himself (Colossians 1:18-20).

There was no one born of Adam's race who could reconcile man to God, because everyone bears the image of Adam, and is a partaker of Adam's sin. "For all have sinned and fall short of the glory of God" (Romans 3:23).

As God said, "Let *Us* make man in *Our* image, according to *Our* likeness" (Genesis 1:26). But that image was destroyed when Adam and Eve chose to believe the devil, that serpent of old, rather than God. With a bite of the forbidden fruit, man was separated from God. Intimacy was exchanged for enmity because man wanted to be as God. And "through one man sin entered into the world" (Romans 5:12), leaving mankind without hope apart from the mercy and grace of God. But "God so loved the world, that He gave His only begotten Son" (John 3:16).

There it is, God's remedy for sin! A whole new race in which we can see the image of God! And how did this "race" come into being? Jesus was begotten of the Father in order to take upon Himself flesh and blood so that He could pay the wages of man's sin, which was death (Romans 6:23).

God gave a prophetic promise in Isaiah 7:14: "The Lord Himself will give you a sign: Behold, a virgin will be with child and bear a son, and she will call His name Immanuel." A virgin was to conceive? But that is impossible! It takes a sperm and an egg to make a child. Yes, Beloved, it does!

When the angel of the Lord told Mary she was going to "conceive in [her] womb and bear a son" who "will be great and will be called the Son of the Most High," she asked, "How can this be, since I am a virgin?" (Luke 1:31,32,34). The angel had the answer: "The Holy Spirit will come upon you, and the power of the Most High will overshadow you; and for that reason the holy offspring shall be called the Son of God....For nothing will be impossible with God" (Luke 1:35,37).

There it was—a promise of God, a provision of another Adam, the last Adam, who would become "a life-giving spirit" (1 Corinthians 15:45). The first Adam brought death, but the last Adam provided life. And who was this last Adam? He was "'Immanuel,' which translated means, 'GOD WITH US'" (Matthew 1:23). He was "the only begotten from the Father, full of grace and truth" (John 1:14). He was the exact representation of God's nature, the Son of God and Man who would pay for our sins and reconcile us to God. O worship Him!

# 63

*Jesus is God because He is the Word, explaining the Father as the I AM.* I want to make sure you have a very clear understanding of the great significance of this point over the next several readings.

I want us to look at John 8:24 and other related passages that will help us understand the full implication of this statement from the mouth of our Lord: "Therefore I said to you that you will die in your sins; for unless you believe that I am *He;* you will die in your sins." You will notice that "He" is in italics because it was added by the translators. The text actually reads, "Unless you believe that I am, you will die in your sins." The "I am" in this verse is called the *egō eimi* because those are the Greek words which were translated "I am."

Let's look at the two other uses of the *egō eimi* in this chapter. The first is in John 8:28: "When you lift up the Son of Man, then you will know that I am *He,* and I do nothing on My own initiative, but I speak these things as the Father taught Me." The second is in John 8:58: "Jesus said to them, 'Truly, truly, I say to you, before Abraham was born, I am.'" After this last statement, the Jews "picked up stones to throw at Him, but Jesus hid Himself and went out of the temple" (John 8:59). Why did the Jews want to stone Him? Understand that and you will see the significance of Jesus' claim of being I AM.

# 64

When Moses met God at the burning bush and received his commission to be God's spokesman before Pharaoh, he asked God a question: "'Behold, I am going to the sons of Israel, and I will say to them, "The God of your fathers has sent me to you." Now they may say to me, "What is His name?' What shall I say to them?' God said to Moses, 'I AM WHO I AM'; and He said, 'Thus you shall say to the sons of Israel, "I AM has sent me to you."' God, furthermore, said to Moses, 'Thus you shall say to the sons of Israel, "The LORD, the God of your fathers, the God of Abraham, the God of Isaac, and the God of Jacob, has sent me to you." This is My name forever, and this is My memorial-name to all generations'" (Exodus 3:13-15).

The Jews wanted to stone Jesus when He said, "Before Abraham was born, I am" (John 8:58). They understood clearly that Jesus was claiming to be God. They knew that I AM was the memorial-name of God to all generations, and they believed Jesus was blaspheming the name of God. They did not believe He was God.

On another occasion, when Jesus said, "I and the Father are one," the Jews again wanted to stone Him. "Jesus answered them, 'I showed you many good works from the Father; for which of them are you stoning Me?' The Jews answered Him, 'For a good work we do not stone

You, but for blasphemy; and because You, being a man, make Yourself out to be God'" (John 10:30-33).

Because the Jews were blind to the fact that Jesus truly was God, that He was equal with the Father and the exact representation of the Father, they viewed His claim to be I AM as blasphemy. Their beliefs gave them every right to stone Him. They knew the Law said, "Moreover, the one who blasphemes the name of the LORD shall surely be put to death; all the congregation shall certainly stone him. The alien as well as the native, when he blasphemes the Name, shall be put to death" (Leviticus 24:16).

Jesus had laid hold of "the Name." That they understood without doubt. O Beloved, the question is, "Do you know that Jesus claimed to be God?" Jehovah's Witnesses claim that in John 10:33 the Jews were not saying that Jesus was making Himself out to be God but *a* god. Don't believe that diluted reasoning! The Jews wouldn't have tried to stone a man for that. They understood that Jesus was taking for Himself the memorial-name of God—I AM. But because they refused to believe in the deity of Jesus Christ, they would die in their sins. They would never know life.

What about you, Beloved? Will you die in your sins, or do you believe that Jesus is I AM, God Himself?

# 65

$O$f all the names of God, none is reverenced more than "Jehovah." This name is a substitute for *Yahweh,* the proper name for God. *Yahweh,* or the tetragrammaton *YHWH,* has been referred to as the great and terrible name of God. Because of Exodus 20:7, which says, "You shall not take the name of the LORD your God in vain, for the LORD will not leave him unpunished who takes His name in vain," and because of Leviticus 24:16, which pronounced the death sentence on anyone who blasphemed the name of the LORD, the Jews were even afraid to pronounce or use the name *Yahweh.* Therefore, they substituted *Jehovah* for *Yahweh* or *YHWH.*

As you read through the Old Testament, you will find LORD all in capital letters in most versions. This translation represents some 6400 occurrences of *YHWH.* Where *YHWH* is linked with *Adon* or *Adhōnāy, YHWH* will be translated "God." There are about 315 of these combinations which are usually translated "Lord GOD."[7] You can see an example of this usage in Genesis 15:2. *Adon* or *Adhōnāy* is the name of God meaning "Lord" and is written with lowercase letters except for the *L.*

Now, Beloved, I have shared all this for a purpose. First, I want you to learn more and more about our Father's infallible Word. But I also want these insights to impact the way you live. Knowledge is not to be gained just for the sake of knowledge, but for the sake of holiness. Once you really understand what God is revealing through His name—I AM or Jehovah—you should be liberated from any fear that you will ever find yourself in a situation where you feel you cannot cope. That's enough to keep one reading, isn't it?

Now then, let me review what I have just said before I give you more encouraging news, truths that will bless you immensely. So, as I tell my Precept students, "Hangeth thou in there."

1. *YHWH* or *Yahweh* is translated "LORD" in the Old Testament and written in uppercase letters, although the *L* is larger. However, when this word is combined with *Adon* or *Adhōnāy*, it will be translated "Lord GOD."

2. From about the twelfth century on, the Jews referred to *YHWH* as *Jehovah*. They used the word *Jehovah* instead of *Yahweh* because they felt it too holy to pronounce. Or they were afraid that they might in some way use this name in vain and thus blaspheme the name of the LORD.[8]

# 66

$\mathcal{G}$od's memorial-name, I AM, is closely related to God's personal name, *YHWH.* In Exodus 3:14, "AM" is the Hebrew[9] word *havah,* which means "to be." *Jah,* one of the names of God, is the present tense of the verb "to be." Therefore, it corresponds to "I AM." *Jehovah* then would correspond to "I AM WHO I AM," which is how God responded to Moses when he asked God's name (Exodus 3:14).[10]

When God says that His name is "I AM," He is showing Himself as Jehovah, the Self-existent One. For us He is, "I AM, I am everything you will ever need." To which we ought to say, "Hallelujah," which means "Praise be to *Jah* [God]." The name I AM, *Jehovah,* reveals God as the One who is able to supply all your needs through Christ Jesus your Lord. As the Self-existent One, He can never be confronted by a claim He cannot meet—as long, of course, as it is according to His will and not in violation of His character. This, Beloved, is why David could write: "The LORD is my shepherd, I shall not want" (Psalm 23:1).

Now then, reason with me for a moment. We have also seen that Jesus is I AM, the *egō eimi. Eimi* in the Greek means "to be, to exist, or to have existence or being." Therefore, Jesus is the Self-existent One. And if that is true, then life can be found only in Him.

Think back with me for a moment to John 1:4, where, referring to Jesus as the Word, John states, "In Him was life." Jesus has always been. He is eternal. He was in the beginning with God. He is God. Therefore, since Jesus is God, since He is the Self-existent One, life cannot be any place else but in Him. Now then, you can better understand Jesus' statement in John 8:24: "Therefore I said to you that you will die in your sins; for unless you believe that I am *He,* you will die in your sins."

We are born sinners, Beloved, and "the wages of sin is death" (Romans 6:23). "And you were dead in your trespasses and sins....But God, being rich in mercy, because of His great love with which He loved us, even when we were dead in our transgressions, made us alive together with Christ (by grace you have been saved)" (Ephesians 2:1,4,5).

Thus, we see that the only way we can have life is to believe that Jesus is the Christ, the Son of God, the I AM. And when in faith—apart from any works on our part we believe in the Lord Jesus Christ, then the wonderful mystery of the gospel takes place, "which is Christ in you, the hope of glory" (Colossians 1:27). "And the testimony is this, that God has given us eternal life, and this life is in His Son. He who has the Son has the life; he who does not have the Son of God does not have the life" (1 John 5:11,12).

O praise be to Jehovah who has given us everything we need in Christ Jesus. May you run to Him—your I AM—for your every need, asking in His name.

*67*

*O*ften when all is calm and peaceful, the wind of adversity can begin to blow, and we find ourselves caught in a raging storm. Fear strikes our hearts. O Beloved, when times like this are upon you, may you hear Jesus say, "It is I; do not be afraid" (John 6:20).

If you were to read John 6:20 in the Greek, you would find the *egō eimi* again in this passage. A literal translation would read: "I AM; do not be afraid." In the light of what we have seen these past two days, you can appreciate this passage even more, and understand why they didn't have to be afraid. Jesus, the Self-existent One, was there with them. In the sudden storm that caught them in the midst of the sea, Jesus was there. He was adequate for every need that would arise. Oh, how our Lord longed to have His disciples learn this truth! Oh, how He longs to have us absorb this reality! It will not remove us from the storms, but it will enable us to weather them in a great peace that passes all understanding. This same story is recorded in Mark 6:47-52: "When it was evening, the boat was in the middle of the sea, and He was alone on the land. Seeing them straining at the oars, for the wind was against them, at about the fourth watch of the night He came to them, walking on the sea....They supposed that it was a ghost, and cried out; for they all saw Him and were terrified. But immediately He spoke with them and said to them, 'Take courage; it is I [I AM—*egō eimi*], do not be afraid.' Then He got into the boat with them, and the wind stopped;

and they were utterly astonished, for they had not gained any insight from the incident of the loaves, but their heart was hardened."

What was the insight they should have gained from the loaves of bread and the fish that Jesus had just multiplied in order to feed the multitude? They should have recognized that Jesus was the Christ, the Son of God, that He was the all-sufficient, self-existent God. They should have noted that He was the One who could and would meet all their needs.

Yet what happened? In the midst of the storm, they forgot what they had seen their God do in a previous situation. O Beloved, have you ever gone through a trial experiencing His all-sufficient grace, only to hit the next storm and totally forget how you made it through the first storm with Jesus "in your boat"? Always remember, dear friend, who is in the boat with you!

# 68

$\mathcal{T}$rials do not come into your life by happenstance, Beloved. Your Sovereign Father, who has you in His hands, filters trials first through His fingers of love. No storm could arise if you were not able to weather it. Can you hear what I am saying, or is your mind closed? Have you become insensitive to who God is and what your Lord Jesus has wrought for you?

After the feeding of the 5000, the disciples set out to cross the Sea of Galilee, and "the sea began to be stirred up because a strong wind was blowing" (John 6:18). They "had not gained any insight from the incident of the loaves, but their heart was hardened" (Mark 6:52) or "their mind was closed."[11]

In Mark 8, we find the disciples once again in a boat on the Sea of Galilee. This time, however, the trial takes a different form. Now they have no bread. They forgot it. Yet look who is in the boat with them! Jesus the One who is the Bread of Life, who fed a multitude, who calmed a storm, and who said, "I AM; be not afraid." The Scripture continues: "They had forgotten to take bread, and did not have more than one loaf in the boat with them. And He was giving orders to them, saying, 'Watch out! Beware of the leaven of the Pharisees and the leaven of Herod.' They began to discuss with one another the fact that they had no bread" (8:14-16).

Can you imagine, Beloved? Here is their Lord trying to teach them valuable truths, and they are missing it because they are occupied with the need of the moment. Have you ever missed what God was trying to teach you because you were so occupied with the need rather than with the One who supplies all your needs? "And Jesus aware of this, said to them, 'Why do you discuss the fact that you have no bread? Do you not yet see or understand? Do you have a hardened heart? Having eyes, do you not see? And having ears, do you not hear? And do you not remember, when I broke the five loaves for the five thousand, how many baskets full of broken pieces you picked up?' They said to Him, 'Twelve.' 'When I broke the seven for the four thousand, how many large baskets full of broken pieces did you pick up?' And they said to Him, 'Seven.' And He was saying to them, 'Do you not yet understand?'" (Mark 8:17-21).

What did our Lord want them to understand? He wanted them to remember He was everything they would ever need and much more. There was no situation of life or circumstance that would arise but what He, Jehovah, was there in the boat with them. He was able not only to meet their needs abundantly but also to calm the storm and bring them safely to shore.

O give glory to I AM—"to Him who is able to do far more abundantly beyond all that we ask or think" (Ephesians 3:20). And in your next storm, don't forget who He is!

*69*

$\mathcal{N}$ot only do we know that Jesus is God because He is eternal and because He, as the Word, explained the Father as the radiance of His glory, as the exact representation of His nature, and as the "I AM." We also know that Jesus is God because He is one with the Father. This truth brings us to the next point of our outline: He is the Word, explaining the Father, as being one with the Father.

When Jesus said, "I and the Father are one" (John 10:30), He used the neuter form of *one*—*hen* in the Greek, meaning "one in essence." Had Jesus used the root word *heis* instead of *hen,* He would have been referring to Himself and the Father as numerically one, or one person. "Sabellius, a second-century heretic and the forerunner of the Unitarians, taught that Jesus was only a radiation, a manifestation of God."[12] Yet John's use of *hen* clearly dispels this.

Jesus was showing us that while He and the Father were two separate personalities, they were one in essence—in their nature, in their attributes. And the Jews understood exactly what Jesus was saying. There was no question on their part that He was proclaiming Himself as God. They felt Jesus was guilty of blasphemy, and they wanted to stone Him.

O Beloved, I cannot tell you how vital it is that you know these things. Study well. Make notes of these points in your Bible. Then when you encounter someone who does not believe in the deity of Jesus Christ and who is trying to persuade you to join his or her sect, you can be used by God to show this person the truth. You may become God's instrument to turn someone from darkness to light, from the power of Satan to the kingdom of God! Have you ever had the joy of being used of God in this way? Dear friend, it is so awesome! Get prepared and watch God use you.

In his book *The Legacy of Jesus,* John MacArthur makes this statement: "The single, central, most important issue about Jesus is the question of His deity. Everyone who studies about Jesus must confront the issue, because of His claims to be God. C.S. Lewis has observed that 'the one thing we must not say' about Jesus is that He is a 'great moral teacher' but not God: 'A man who was merely a man and said the sort of things Jesus said would not be a great moral teacher. He would either be a lunatic—on a level with the man who says he is a poached egg—or else he would be the Devil of Hell. You must make your choice. Either this man was, and is, the Son of God; or else a madman or something worse.'"[13]

Think on these things, Beloved.

# 70

*H*ave you ever desired a greater intimacy with the Father, yet felt that God was too awesome and too far removed for you to enjoy that type of relationship? Has your vision of God been of a Person who seemed so holy that you felt you could not endure His presence? Or have you ever felt a paralyzing fear in respect to God?

O Beloved, if you will get to know Jesus Christ in an intimate way through studying and meditating upon the Word, you will find this intimacy dispelling your misconceptions of God. Because Jesus was one in essence with the Father, He could say, "He who sees Me sees the One who sent Me" (John 12:45). As you see "as in a mirror the glory of the Lord" (2 Corinthians 3:18), you will find yourself more and more enraptured with the Father heart of God. You will become more and more secure in your knowledge of Him.

Remember, Jesus came to explain the Father. In John 14, we find our Lord preparing the disciples for His departure. They are about to go through the trauma of seeing the One for whom they have left all die an ignominious death on a cross. And until His resurrection, their grief will be almost unbearable. For although He told them of His death and resurrection, it was almost as if they were deaf. They could not comprehend the horror of what He was communicating.

Thus, we hear our Lord in the Upper Room assuring them that He is going to His Father's house to prepare a place for them. He tells them that if He goes away, He will surely return for them. It is at this point that Thomas asks, "'Lord, we do not know where You are going, how do we know the way?' Jesus said to him, 'I am [*egō eimi*] the way, and the truth, and the life; no one comes to the Father, but through Me. If you had known Me, you would have known My Father also; from now on you know Him, and have seen Him'" (John 14:5-7).

There it is once again. *When you get to know Jesus, you will get to know the Father, for They are one in essence.*

Philip said to Him, "'Lord, show us the Father, and it is enough for us.' Jesus said to him, 'Have I been so long with you, and yet you have not come to know Me, Philip? He who has seen Me has seen the Father; how can you say, "Show us the Father?" Do you not believe that I am in the Father, and the Father is in Me?'" (John 14:8-10).

I leave you, Beloved, with Jesus' question to Philip. Consider it His question to you: Do you believe Jesus is one with the Father and, therefore, that He is God? And what are you doing in order to get to know your Father God intimately as your Friend?

# 71

$\mathcal{W}$hat is the ultimate goal, the supreme purpose, of your life? This is a very crucial question, because those without goals usually live purposeless lives that are wasted and often regretted. Don't ever forget that you will be held accountable before your God for how you spend your life. It is He who brought you into existence.

Fulfillment comes from knowing that you have achieved your purpose. What is the ultimate goal, the supreme purpose, of your life? Write out your answer in your notebook.

As the day of our Lord's crucifixion hovered as a dark cloud over the disciples, in their presence Jesus lifted up His eyes to heaven and said, "Father, the hour has come; glorify Your Son, that the Son may glorify You" (John 17:1). To the very end of His life, Jesus' desire was to glorify the Father, to give an exact estimate of who the Father was. As the curtain of death was about to go down, ending the drama of a life lived with one ultimate goal, Jesus could say, "I glorified You on the earth, having accomplished the work which You have given Me to do" (John 17:4). And because He achieved this goal, there was an encore: the resurrection!

And what was Jesus' desire for those He would leave behind? It was that they too would achieve oneness: "The glory which You have given Me I have given to them, that they may be one, just as We are one; I in them, and You in Me, that they may be perfected in unity, so that the world may know that You sent Me, and loved them, even as You have loved Me" (John 17:22,23).

Again we see Jesus' deity confirmed, as He refers over and over to His oneness with the Father. Don't miss the fact that this oneness gave Him His purpose in life, and then held Him to this purpose. Even in the agony of Gethsemane He prayed, "My Father, if it is possible, let this cup pass from Me; yet not as I will, but as You will" (Matthew 26:39).

O dear child of God, may you so make oneness with the Father your goal that you will realize daily that your ultimate goal too is to glorify Him on earth by accomplishing the work He has given you to do. "For we are His workmanship, created in Christ Jesus for good works, which God prepared beforehand so that we would walk in them" (Ephesians 2:10).

## 72

*I*f you are going to allow the Word of God to speak for itself, without twisting it or distorting it, you must believe that Jesus is one with the Father, God in the flesh. In Colossians 2:9 we read: "For in Him all the fullness of Deity dwells in bodily form." God said it again and again as men moved by the Spirit of God wrote for us the Word of God. It is there in the Old Testament, in the Gospels, in Acts, in the Epistles, and in Revelation: Jesus is God.

Philippians gives us one of the clearest descriptions of the deity and humanity of Jesus Christ in the form of a word of exhortation to those in Philippi. Let's look at it verse by verse, and I will explain it as we go along. Don't miss the exhortation: "Have this attitude in yourselves which was also in Christ Jesus, who, although He existed in the form of God, did not regard equality with God a thing to be grasped" (Philippians 2:5,6). There it is again: Jesus is equal with God, the same as God in essence.

The Greek word for *form* is *morphē*, and I don't want you to miss its wonderful depth of meaning. Therefore, I want to share what W.E. Vine has to say in his *Expository Dictionary of Old and New Testament Words*: "*Morphē* denotes 'the special or characteristic form or feature' of a person or thing....An excellent definition of the word is that of Gifford: '*morphē* is therefore properly the nature or essence, not in the abstract, but as actually subsisting in the individual, and retained as long as the individual itself exists.'...Thus in the passage before us [Philippians 2:6] *morphē Theou* is the Divine nature actually and inseparably subsisting in the Person of Christ....The true meaning of *morphē* in the expression 'form of God' is confirmed by its recurrence in the corresponding phrase, 'form of a servant.' It is universally admitted that the two phrases are directly antithetical, and that 'form' must therefore have the same sense in both" (from Gifford, *The Incarnation,* 16,19,39).[14]

Because Jesus was God, He continued to be God even when He took the form of a servant.

# 73

*A*lthough Jesus was God, He "did not regard equality with God a thing to be grasped" (Philippians 2:6). He did not hang on His right to be God in a way that kept Him from taking upon Himself the form of a bond-servant. Here is the exhortation to us as children of God. We are to be willing to humble ourselves, even as Jesus our Lord did. Although He retained His deity at all times, Jesus was willing to lay aside His rights as God in order that He might be "made in the likeness of men. Being found in appearance as a man, He humbled Himself by becoming obedient to the point of death, even death on a cross" (Philippians 2:7,8).

There was no more shameful or painful death than that of crucifixion. And yet God the Son was willing to obey God and serve us in this way, so that we might not have to die in our sins but could have eternal life.

As you read the Gospel of John, you will see two titles used of Jesus repeatedly. He is called "Son of God," which shows His deity, and "Son of Man," which shows His humanity. As we see Jesus as the Son of God and the Son of Man in Philippians, we are convicted in our hearts that we must have the attitude of our Lord.

After all, if He who is God was willing to become a bond-servant that He might lay down His life for us, then shouldn't we be willing to lay down our lives, our personal rights, for the sake of others? How can we cling to our puny rights when Jesus, the Son of God, was willing to empty Himself of His just rights as God?

O Beloved, in a time when there is so much emphasis on self, on being number one, how vital it is that you be "firmly rooted" in Him, "built up in Him and established in your faith, just as you were instructed, and overflowing with gratitude. See to it that no one takes you captive through philosophy and empty deception, according to the tradition of men, according to the elementary principles of the world, rather than according to Christ. For in Him all the fullness of Deity dwells in bodily form, and in Him you have been made complete" (Colossians 2:7-10).

In the light of what we have learned, why don't you examine your relationship with other people? Is there anything you are doing from selfishness or empty conceit? Are you regarding yourself as more important than others? Do you care only about your own interests, or are you seeking ways that you might please your mate, your children, family members, and fellow Christians? Who is number one in your life—you or God? If God, then others will come before you.

# 74

*A*nyone who possesses the sovereign rights to raise the dead, to judge mankind, and to receive honor that belongs to God must certainly be God. In John 5 we see a magnificent portrait of the Son in His relationship to the Father: Jesus Christ is God because He is the possessor of the sovereign rights of God.

Let's look at how the Son explains to a group of angry Jews one of His sovereign rights as the Son of God: "For this reason therefore the Jews were seeking all the more to kill Him, because He not only was breaking the Sabbath, but also was calling God His own Father, making Himself equal with God" (John 5:18). It is at this point that Jesus refers to Himself over and over as "the Son," showing what the Son can do because He is the Son. He explains to them that a day is coming when all the dead shall be raised and that He has the right to act as the Son of God to call them forth: "Truly, truly, I say to you, an hour is coming and now is, when the dead will hear the voice of the Son of God, and those who hear will live....Do not marvel at this; for an hour is coming, in which all who are in the tombs will hear His voice, and will come forth; those who did the good deeds to a resurrection of life, those who committed the evil deeds to a resurrection of judgment" (John 5:25,28,29).

Jesus makes His statement regarding the resurrection of the dead in John 5, and then in John 11 gives them a foretaste of His authority over death, as He "cried out with a loud voice, 'Lazarus, come forth'"

(11:43). Lazarus, who had been dead four days, came forth suddenly. He must have been propelled, because he certainly was unable to walk in his grave clothes! Those who witnessed the event knew that Jesus was the Son of God. If Jesus had not specifically said, "Lazarus," I am sure that all the dead would have come forth in obedience to the voice of God!

Not only will Jesus raise the dead, but as God He will also judge them (John 5:22). The Father "gave Him authority to execute judgment, because He is the Son of Man" (John 5:27). And this is only right, for Jesus demonstrated that man could live in obedience to God. And finally, all will "honor the Son even as they honor the Father. He who does not honor the Son does not honor the Father who sent Him" (John 5:23).

# 15

$\mathcal{H}$ave you ever wondered why people are so eager to embrace evolution and so adamantly opposed to the biblical account of creation? I think the root of this paradox is pride, and the root of pride is sin. It is turning to our "own way" (Isaiah 53:6) and refusing to submit to the ownership of God. After all, didn't that "serpent of old who is called the devil and Satan" (Revelation 12:9) offer Eve a way to be her own god if she would eat of the forbidden fruit of the tree of the knowledge of good and evil? Didn't Satan tell Eve that in the day she ate of the fruit from that tree she would be like God, knowing good and evil? Of course! It is all recorded for us in Genesis 3. Man did not want God to rule over him. He wanted to be his own god.

It is this attitude that causes people to reject the Bible's idea of creation. For if we are created, if there is a cause behind this universe, if we did not evolve from a lower form of life but are a unique and special creation, then there has to be a Creator. And you have to spell *Creator* with a capital *C*, for He has to be other than we are. And if we have a Creator, then we are accountable to live in obedience to Him, because we owe our existence to Him. The Word of God states: "In the beginning God created the heavens and the earth....Then God said, 'Let Us make man in Our image....' God created man in His own image, in the image of God He created him; male and female He created them....The LORD God formed man of dust from the ground, and breathed into his nostrils the breath of life; and man became a living being….The LORD God commanded the man…" (Genesis 1:1,26,27; 2:7,16).

From Genesis, it is clear that the Creator is the LORD God, YHWH Elohim. And who is this YHWH Elohim? Well, a careful reading of Genesis 1:26 indicates that YHWH is more than one: "Then God said, 'Let *Us* make man in *Our* image.'" This fact, of course, brings us to the third major point of our outline on the deity of Jesus Christ: *Jesus Christ is God because He is Creator.*

O Beloved, do not grow weary of our subject. In all probability you know without a shadow of a doubt that Jesus is God. However, there are so many who do not know, and their tactics are subtle in their attempts to deceive.

May we never need Paul's word of admonition: "For if one comes and preaches another Jesus whom we have not preached, or you receive a different spirit which you have not received, or a different gospel which you have not accepted, you bear this beautifully" (2 Corinthians 11:4).

# 76

*W*hen God said, "Let Us make man in Our image," Jesus Christ was right there with Him. In John 1:3 we read: "All things came into being through Him, and apart from Him nothing came into being that has come into being."

In Paul's epistle to the Colossians, he establishes the fact that Jesus "is the image of the invisible God, the firstborn of all creation" (1:15). Therefore, Jesus is not part of creation; He is Creator. Thus, Paul goes on to say, "For by Him all things were created, both in the heavens and on earth, visible and invisible, whether thrones or dominions or rulers or authorities—all things have been created through Him and for Him" (1:16).

Yet another epistle leaves us with no doubt that Jesus is Creator, and that is Hebrews. This is a difficult but magnificent book which Christians desperately need to understand if they are going to endure trials without throwing away their confidence in Jesus Christ. It was written to believers who were suffering for their faith and who needed to understand the importance of holding fast, not drifting away but going on to maturity by coming boldly to the throne of grace and finding help in the time of need (4:14-16) from their great high priest, the Lord Jesus Christ, who ever lives to make intercession for them and who is able to save them forever (7:25).

In Hebrews 1, Jesus is established as being "much better than the angels" and the One of whom the Father said: "LET ALL THE ANGELS OF

GOD WORSHIP HIM." The angels were ministers of God, "but of the Son He says, 'YOUR THRONE, O GOD, IS FOREVER AND EVER.'…and 'YOU, LORD, IN THE BEGINNING LAID THE FOUNDATION OF THE EARTH, AND THE HEAVENS ARE THE WORKS OF YOUR HANDS; THEY WILL PERISH, BUT YOU REMAIN…YOUR YEARS WILL NOT COME TO AN END'" (Hebrews 1:4,6,8,10-12, quoting from Psalm 45:6,7; 102:25-27).

Dear one, Jesus is your Creator—worthy of your obedience, your submission. If you fight this, you will be fighting God. And no man fights God and wins—you only die in your sins.

*77*

*A*nd I saw the dead, the great and the small, standing before the throne" (Revelation 20:12). The rich and poor, powerful and weak, great and small, educated and ignorant, red, yellow, black, white, all have one thing in common: They are dead. Not just physically dead, but spiritually dead. Men, women, and teenagers who are twice dead, "for whom the black darkness has been reserved forever" (Jude 13). Men, women, and teenagers who do not possess the Lord Jesus Christ.

And because they do not, they stand before God's throne to be forever condemned to the lake of fire. This lake of fire is "the second death" (Revelation 20:14). God prepared the lake of fire "for the devil and his angels," not for man (Matthew 25:41). Yet it shall become the eternal abode of all those whose names are "not found written in the book of life" (Revelation 20:15).

It is not God's will that any should perish. He wants you to come to repentance, to have a change of mind about who Jesus Christ is. He wants all to believe that He is God, Jehovah, so they will not have to die in their sins. But multitudes do not come to Him that they might have life. *In Jesus is life*, and in Him alone. So now we come to the fourth major point of our outline on the deity of Jesus Christ: *Jesus Christ is God because in Him is life.*

In John 1:4 we read: "In Him was life, and the life was the Light of men." In Genesis 2:7 it says man was mere dust until "the LORD

God…breathed into his nostrils the breath of life; and man became a living being [soul]."

There is no life apart from Jesus Christ, for life abides in Him alone. Jesus is "the bread of God…which comes down out of heaven, and gives life to the world" (John 6:33). "Everyone who beholds the Son and believes in Him will have eternal life," and Jesus Himself "will raise him up on the last day" (John 6:40).

Believers will not stand at the Great White Throne Judgment of God. Because they have believed that Jesus is God and have accepted Him as Lord and Savior, they have also accepted His finished work at Calvary where the Lamb of God, the Son of Man, died in their stead and covered their sins. He has breathed into them the breath of life, and sealed them "in Him with the Holy Spirit of promise, who is given as a pledge of our inheritance, with a view to the redemption of God's own possession, to the praise of His glory" (Ephesians 1:13,14). They will never see the second death, for God has given them eternal life, "and this life is in His Son" (1 John 5:11).

Jesus stood before Martha, the grieving sister of Lazarus who had been dead four days, and said, "I am the resurrection and the life; he who believes in Me will live even if he dies, and everyone who lives and believes in Me will never die" (John 11:25,26). The second death has no power over those who have believed Jesus is God.

# 78

The news came! The tomb was empty! His body had not been stolen. Jesus was alive! He had appeared to some of the disciples, and they said to Thomas, one of the twelve, "'We have seen the Lord!' But he said to them, 'Unless I see in His hands the imprint of the nails, and put my finger into the place of the nails, and put my hand into His side, I will not believe'" (John 20:25). It was hard for Thomas to believe. Jesus had been so dead! He had seen those spikes suspending his Hope by the hands. He had watched the spear being thrust into the breast upon which John had leaned. He had seen blood and water pouring forth from His broken heart through the gaping hole. Jesus had bled like an ordinary man and had died as all men do. He had been buried like everyone else. Jesus couldn't be alive, could He?

It had been a special three years. A time filled with hope and purpose that had come to an end. Faith was gone, buried in a tomb. Thomas could not resurrect it unless he could put his fingers in the nail holes of a living Jesus and unless He could put his hand in Jesus' side. Only then would Thomas believe: "After eight days His disciples were again inside, and Thomas with them. Jesus came, the doors having been shut, and stood in their midst, and said, 'Peace be with you.' Then He said to Thomas, 'Reach here with your finger, and see My hands; and reach here your hand and put it into My side; and do not be unbelieving, but believing.' Thomas answered and said to Him, 'My Lord and my God!'" (John 20:26-28).

Thomas believed. He saw Jesus for who He was—his Lord and his God. It is this confession that brings us to the fifth and last major point of our outline on the deity of Jesus Christ: *Jesus Christ is God because He is Lord.*

Once again we need to turn to that classic passage on the deity and humanity of Jesus Christ, Philippians 2. This time I want to take you beyond the humiliation of Jesus Christ at Calvary to that which is yet to come, His exaltation by the Father: "Being found in appearance as a man, He humbled Himself by becoming obedient to the point of death, even death on a cross. For this reason also, God highly exalted Him, and bestowed on Him the name which is above every name, so that at the name of Jesus EVERY KNEE SHOULD BOW, of those who are in heaven and on earth and under the earth, and that every tongue will confess that Jesus Christ is Lord, to the glory of God the Father" (Philippians 2:8-11).

O Beloved, if God the Father will cause every knee to bow and every tongue to confess that Jesus is Lord, who are we to contradict God? Know this: If you refuse to bow now and confess Jesus as your Lord and your God, you will someday confess who He is. But if your physical death comes first, it will be too late for you.

# 79

*T*here is a superficial faith, and there is a real faith. Real faith is seen over the proverbial long haul. Real faith endures. It shows in the trials of life, in the times of testing. Faith can be *proclaimed* as real, but it isn't *seen* as genuine until it is tested. Real faith is proven faith that stands the test.

As you read through the Gospel of John, you see two different types of believing which result in either a superficial faith or the genuine thing. Let me give you an example of what I mean, and then let me share with you what I believe makes the difference between the superficial and the real. In John 2:23-25 we read: "Now when He was in Jerusalem at the Passover, during the feast, many believed in His name, observing His signs which He was doing. But Jesus, on His part, was not entrusting Himself to them, for He knew all men, and because He did not need anyone to testify concerning man, for He Himself knew what was in man."

Jesus knew that many people were convinced by the signs He performed, but were not genuinely convinced about Jesus Himself, for He would not entrust Himself to them.

In John 6, we see the same thing happening. Jesus gathered quite a group of followers because of the signs He performed. Some were even considered disciples, until they heard His hard sayings. "As a result of this many of His disciples withdrew and were not walking with Him anymore" (John 6:66).

When Jesus asked the twelve if they wanted to go away also, "Simon Peter answered Him, 'Lord, to whom shall we go? You have words of eternal life. We have believed and have come to know that You are the Holy One of God'" (John 6:68,69). As the spokesman, Peter was telling Jesus that it was more than the signs they had believed. It was His words. It was His Person. They were convinced that Jesus was God and that He had given them the truth of God. Peter was saying, in essence, that their faith was the real thing. It wasn't based on signs. Their faith rested in a true knowledge and commitment to the words and Person of Jesus Christ.

Yet while Peter was speaking, Jesus pointed out that one of the twelve did not have genuine faith. He knew that in the time of testing, Judas' faith would fail.

# *80*

Some people believe in signs and in the Jesus who performs them. Others believe in Jesus for who He is, not just for what He performs.

Some will follow Him as long as He performs the way they want Him to. Others will follow Him, no matter what happens.

Some possess Jesus. Others Jesus possesses. Therein lies the difference between superficial and real faith. It is all wrapped up in believing in who He is.

Genuine, saving faith accepts that Jesus is the Christ, the promised Messiah of whom the Old Testament prophesied. Genuine, saving faith accepts the fact that Jesus is the Son of God and, thereby, all that God is. If I am going to acknowledge Jesus as God, then I must be willing to live accordingly. If Jesus is God, then He has a right to rule over me.

Paul calls real faith "the obedience of faith" (Romans 1:5). If Jesus is God, then I am not my own. There is to be a total commitment of myself to God so that He possesses me. "Do you not know that your body is a temple of the Holy Spirit who is in you, whom you have from God, and that you are not your own? For you have been bought with a price: therefore glorify God in your body" (1 Corinthians 6:19,20). It is recognizing Jesus for who He is and accepting and submitting to who He is—my Lord and my God—that brings genuine faith.

Real faith is not mere intellectual assent. Genuine faith is comprised of a firm conviction based on knowledge, a personal surrender, and conduct inspired by such a surrender. Salvation is surrendering your-self to God and to what He has revealed about His Son.

It is all pure grace. There is absolutely nothing that you as a desti-tute sinner can do to save yourself. In genuine faith, you simply put your trust in all that Jesus Christ is and in all that He has accomplished in His death, burial, and resurrection.

As you read Paul's words, notice that Jesus is Lord because He is God: "'The word is near you, in your mouth and in your heart'—that is, the word of faith which we are preaching, that if you confess with your mouth Jesus as Lord, and believe in your heart that God raised Him from the dead, you will be saved; for with the heart a person believes, resulting in righteousness, and with the mouth he confesses, resulting in salvation. For the Scripture says, 'WHOEVER BELIEVES IN HIM WILL NOT BE DISAPPOINTED.' For there is no distinction between Jew and Greek; for the same Lord is Lord of all, abounding in riches for all who call on Him; for 'WHOEVER WILL CALL UPON THE NAME OF THE LORD WILL BE SAVED'" (Romans 10:8-13).

Genuine faith does not rest on signs or benefits, but on the Savior who is the Lord Jesus Christ, God incarnate.

# 81

*J*esus once turned to a group of Jews "who had believed Him" and told them what constituted genuine discipleship, genuine salvation: "If you continue in My word, then you are truly disciples of Mine; and you will know the truth, and the truth will make you free" (John 8:31,32). Just before this He had said to them, "Unless you believe that I am He, you will die in your sins" (8:24).

True faith produces a changed life because it produces obedience. Obedience and belief go hand in hand, just as disobedience and unbelief go hand in hand. Many Scriptures teach this truth, but I will simply give you Hebrews 3:18,19 to show you the parallel between disobedience and unbelief: "And to whom did He swear that they would not enter His rest, but to those who were disobedient? So we see that they were not able to enter because of unbelief."

Now when I say real faith produces obedience, I do not mean that a true child of God will not sin. However, the true child of God will change in respect to sin. "How shall we who died to sin still live in it?" (Romans 6:2).

A true believer's life changes in respect to sin because he has believed in Him! (See 1 John 3:7-10.) A person must believe that Jesus is God if he wants to be saved. And if I acknowledge Jesus as God, along with all this implies, I am turning from sin, or running my own life, to Jesus, who as God has the right to run my life. If I acknowledge

Jesus as God, then I am going to believe what He says. I am going to know the truth, and the truth will make me free (John 8:32).

Also, although I was a slave to sin, for "everyone who commits sin is the slave of sin" (John 8:34), I will now be free from slavery to sin, for "if the Son makes you free, you will be free indeed" (John 8:36). This freedom comes—as we read in 1 John 3—because His seed abides in me, and I cannot practice habitual sin (as a way of life) because I am born of God. Here again is the difference between genuine and superficial faith.

# 82

$\mathcal{P}$lease read John 8:31-59. We find our Lord making very strong statements to some Jews who had believed in Him. From the context of this passage, it seems that theirs was a superficial belief, for Jesus said to them:

> If God were your Father, you would love Me, for I proceeded forth and have come from God, for I have not even come on My own initiative, but He sent Me. Why do you not understand what I am saying? It is because you cannot hear My word. You are of your father the devil, and you want to do the desires of your father. He was a murderer from the beginning, and does not stand in the truth because there is no truth in him. Whenever he speaks a lie, he speaks from his own nature, for he is a liar and the father of lies. But because I speak the truth, you do not believe Me. Which one of you convicts Me of sin? If I speak truth, why do you not believe Me? He who is of God hears the words of God; for this reason you do not hear them, because you are not of God (John 8:42-47).

All mankind has one of two fathers—either God or the devil. It is easy to spot some who have the devil as their father, but not all. The religious, those who have a superficial faith, are sometimes hard to discern, for even they are deceived, believing heaven is their home and God is their Father. Let me quote what Lawrence O. Richards says in his *Expository Dictionary of Bible Words:*

> There is counterfeit belief, which exists as a limited trust in Jesus. Counterfeit belief acknowledges that there is something special about Jesus but refuses to accept Scripture's full testimony about him. Saving faith goes beyond limited belief. It recognizes Jesus as Son of God and trusts completely in him as he is unveiled in God's Word. Saving faith demonstrates belief by acting on the words Jesus has spoken (John 8:31-32).
>
> In making a faith commitment, a person considers the evidence and accepts God's testimony about who Jesus is. The one who does not believe may be impressed with the evidence but will hold back from entrusting himself or herself to Jesus.
>
> Yet it is only by believing, as a total commitment of oneself to the Lord, that life can be found. How vital then that we consider the testimony of Scripture, accept it, and believe on the one who speaks words of promise there.
>
> John sees believing as an active, continuing trust in Jesus. The act of believing draws an individual across the dividing line between death and eternal life. That act of faith is described by John as receiving Jesus (John 1:12) and as coming to him (John 6:35), as well as loving him (1 John 4:19).[15]

O Beloved, does this help you to tell real faith from the counterfeit?

# 83

"Your father is the devil. You are doing the deeds of your father." When you hear statements like these, do you imagine someone involved in witchcraft—contacting the dead, offering animal or human sacrifices in a black mass? Or, when you hear of the deeds of the devil, do you think of drug abuse, immorality, pornography, stealing, murder? All of these seem to be obvious deeds of the devil, don't they? They are easy to spot and to define as not being of God.

And yet in the context of Jesus' statements that the Jews' father was the devil and the deeds they were doing were of the devil himself, the devil's deeds are not always blatant. They are not as easily discerned in this passage as those I have just mentioned. And yet, the deeds of the devil have one root source from which every deed springs: "the lie."

"The lie" is that which contradicts truth—*anything* which goes against what the Word of God teaches. It is the nature of the devil to go against the Word of God. Listen again to John 8:44: "You are of your father the devil, and you want to do the desires of your father. He was a murderer from the beginning."

In other words, the devil wanted to destroy Adam and Eve. He wanted them to believe his lie that assured them: "You surely will not die!" (Genesis 3:4). All the time the devil knew that they would die! And die they did—spiritually and later physically. Death entered the world because Adam and Eve believed the devil's lie. The devil was a murderer. He "does not stand in the truth because there is no truth in him. Whenever he speaks a lie [literally, "the lie"], he speaks from his own nature; for he is a liar and the father of lies" (John 8:44). It is the very nature of the devil to lie, to contradict the truth, to deceive men so that they turn from truth. Therefore, every lie that has ever been perpetrated—every contradiction of the truth of God's Word— has its root in the devil, for he is the father of lies, the one who conceives them.

O Beloved, do you realize what God is saying? Everything that contradicts the Word of God has its root in the devil. And the fruit of the root is death, for the devil is a murderer. The Word of God is truth!

Jesus prayed, "Sanctify them in the truth; Your word is truth" (John 17:17). And what is the truth about Jesus Christ? "Unless you believe that I am *He,* you will die in your sins" (John 8:24). If you do not believe that Jesus is God, the devil has murdered you because you believed his lie, and you will spend eternity in the lake of fire. Do you believe?

# 84

*W*ell, beloved friend, it is my prayer that you now have a clear understanding of the deity of Jesus Christ and that you feel confident that you could share the truth of it with another.

Take today and pray through what you've learned. Then write out in your notebook a simple explanation of the deity of Jesus Christ. It will be an exercise to cement in your mind all that you've learned so that you are prepared to "contend earnestly for the faith which was once for all delivered to the saints" (Jude 3).

Take time too to thank God for His incredible plan of salvation!

# What Happens When You Hear Your Shepherd's Voice?

~

## JOHN 9–11

$85$

*F*or the first time he saw the light of day, and all because of the One who was the Light of the world. According to John 9, the man had been blind from birth. Then Jesus came, spat on the ground, made clay of the spittle, applied it to his eyes, and told him to wash in the pool of Siloam. The man went to the pool blind and came back seeing!

No more would he sit as a beggar. No longer would his life be an object of pity. No longer would he be condemned to darkness. Light had come, and with that light came life! The man believed on the One who removed the veil of blindness from his eyes.

Whenever I read this account, I cannot help but think of how it parallels my life—and the life of every child of God. As I note the amount of space devoted to this incident, I believe that God wanted John to show us a picture of what takes place when a person comes to know the Lord Jesus Christ in a personal way.

The parallels between John 9 and our salvation are many, for we were also once in spiritual darkness. We were each born blind to the glorious light of the gospel of Jesus Christ. Did we not also sit as beggars, poverty-stricken when it came to any righteousness which might cover our spiritual nakedness? And in our blindness, did we not grope through life, unable to see where we were going?

Yet, once we were healed of sin's awful disease, did everyone rejoice with us over the change in our lives? Weren't there some who didn't want to admit that our transformation was a sheer miracle? Didn't many deny that only Jesus Christ could make such a transformation? Didn't people who once accepted us now reject us and want to kick us out of their "fellowship"? Reality was that they, too, were in darkness, but they did not recognize their blindness.

As we continue our devotional study together, I want you to see what it means to belong to the family of God, to be turned from darkness to light, from the power of Satan to the kingdom of God. I want you to know what happens when you hear the voice of your Shepherd and come into His fold, where no one can snatch you from His hand. I want you to behold truths which will loosen death's grave clothes so that you will walk in peace, trusting the One who is the Resurrection and the Life. Finish today's time by reading John 9.

# 86

*I*t is the work of God to do the supernatural! When we recognize our own state of impotence, then God is ready to take over in His all-powerful way. It is not until we come to an awareness of our total poverty of spirit in regard to saving ourselves that we can ever be saved. Jesus said, "Blessed are the poor in spirit, for theirs is the kingdom of heaven" (Matthew 5:3).

There was one thing the blind man of John 9 knew for certain: He was blind and there was no human cure for his blindness. If sight depended on him or any person, he would remain blind. When the disciples passed the blind man sitting outside the Temple, they asked Jesus, "'Rabbi, who sinned, this man or his parents, that he would be born blind?' Jesus answered, 'It was neither that this man sinned, nor his parents; but it was so that the works of God might be displayed in him. We must work the works of Him who sent Me as long as it is day; night is coming when no one can work'" (John 9:2-4).

God was going to do what He alone could do: the supernatural. When the supernatural is done, God is glorified.

O Beloved, are the works of God being displayed in you because you have been saved and are different than you used to be? His supernatural transformation begins: 1) when you see your own impotence; 2) when you realize you cannot change yourself; 3) when you know you cannot commend yourself to God; 4) when you simply take God at His Word and believe Him.

Only then is God able to open your eyes so that you might turn from darkness to light, and from the dominion of Satan to God, and might receive forgiveness of sins and an inheritance among those who have been sanctified by faith in Him (Acts 26:18). As God allowed the blindness of the man so that "the works of God might be displayed in him" (John 9:3), so I believe God allows us to get into the messes we do so we will look to Him in our poverty of spirit and be saved.

Do you know people who think they can straighten up their lives and make it to heaven? O Beloved, they are still blind! Maybe God will use you to introduce them to the Light of the world before the night comes and there is no more opportunity. Pray that they will not be like the Pharisees who thought they could see, but who were blind and whose sin remained.

*87*

$\mathcal{T}$he work of Jesus Christ will always bring division. That is hard for some to accept; they think that when a person comes to know Jesus Christ, he is automatically put at peace with everyone. They misunderstand the announcement of the angels at the birth of Jesus, and hear only, "Peace on earth, good will toward men." In reality, the angels declared, "Glory to God in the highest, and on earth peace among men with whom He is pleased" (Luke 2:14). Or, "On earth peace among men of [His] good pleasure or [His] good will."

Peace on earth is not an automatic by-product of Jesus Christ's first coming to the earth. When Jesus was received as God and Savior, it often resulted in division.

In John 9, you probably noted that Jesus' healing of the blind man brought a division among the people. When the blind man—or anyone—confessed Jesus to be the Christ, they would be "put out of the synagogue" (9:22). To put a Jew out of the synagogue was to cut him off from learning the Word of God and from worshiping with other believers.

Jesus was eager for those who would consider following Him to understand this reality. Thus, He said, "Do not think that I came to bring peace on the earth; I did not come to bring peace, but a sword. For I came to SET A MAN AGAINST HIS FATHER, AND A DAUGHTER AGAINST HER MOTHER, AND A DAUGHTER-IN-LAW AGAINST HER MOTHER-IN-LAW; and A MAN'S ENEMIES WILL BE THE MEMBERS OF HIS HOUSEHOLD. He who loves father or mother more than Me is not worthy of Me; and he who loves son or daughter more than Me is not worthy of Me" (Matthew 10:34-37).

Jesus is God. As God, He must have the preeminence in our lives. Not to give Him this is to be guilty of idolatry. We cannot put anyone or anything in His rightful place in our lives. Thus, following Jesus brings division with anyone who would resent or object to Jesus having first place in your life.

But you may say, "I love my mother, my father, my husband, my child, my in-laws. It grieves me to be at odds with them because I cannot accept their beliefs or follow some of their ways." I understand. The grief of rejection and separation is difficult, but it must not deter you from fully following your Lord and walking in His light.

## 88

 $W$ hen you embrace the Lord Jesus Christ, you embrace the cross. You cannot separate Jesus from Calvary because He was born to die. He was "the Lamb of God who takes away the sin of the world!" (John 1:29). And since "the wages of sin is death" (Romans 6:23), the sin of the world could be taken away only through His death. At His death He became our substitute. Jesus, who knew no sin, was made sin for us "that we might become the righteousness of God in Him" (2 Corinthians 5:21).

It is the cross that brings division. The cross of Calvary separates us from death unto life, from sin unto righteousness, from hell unto heaven, from being under Satan's dominion to being under God's. The cross also separates us from the world and from all who are of the world, whether they are religious or rank sinners. Any who have not believed on the Lord Jesus Christ belong to the world and its system.

What was true of Paul should also be true of us: "But may it never be that I would boast, except in the cross of our Lord Jesus Christ, through which the world has been crucified to me, and I to the world" (Galatians 6:14). Embracing Jesus brings division because the cross is the place where life begins and is to be lived.

In Galatians 2:20, we read: "I have been crucified with Christ; and it is no longer I who live, but Christ lives in me; and the life which I now live in the flesh I live by faith in the Son of God, who loved me and gave Himself up for me." The cross is the place where self-life ends.

The life in which you were once god is over. Your love of self or of others can no longer have preeminence over your love of God. Jesus told those who would follow Him, "If anyone comes to Me, and does not hate his own father and mother and wife and children and brothers and sisters, yes, and even his own life, he cannot be My disciple. Whoever does not carry his own cross and come after Me cannot be My disciple" (Luke 14:26,27).

How prophetically right the Jews were when they said to the man blind from birth, "You are His disciple" (John 9:28), for that was exactly what he was going to become. Although they tried to persuade the blind man that Jesus was a sinner and not the Christ, he knew that Jesus was sent from God. And because the blind man took hold of this truth, "they put him out" of the synagogue (John 9:34). But even that separation could not force him to change his mind about Jesus. "He worshiped Him" (John 9:38).

O Beloved, have you experienced the separation that taking up your cross and following Him brings? Don't despair! You have seen the Light. You are blind no more!

# 89

$\mathcal{N}$ot only did the Jews kick the blind man out of the synagogue, but they also wanted Jesus out of both the synagogue and the Temple. As a matter of fact, the Jews wanted Jesus Christ dead! The Jewish leaders were to be the shepherds of Israel, taking care of the flock of God. Yet they were more concerned about themselves and their own welfare than the welfare of the sheep.

Instead of rejoicing over the healing of this blind son of Israel, they became angry with him because he said that he had been healed by Jesus. Too many were following Jesus and listening to His teachings, and it threatened their power. Jesus violated their interpretation of the Law and broke their traditions. Why, soon the Jewish leaders might lose their hold over the people, and eventually their place of ruler-ship under the Romans! Now here before them stood a witness who insisted that Jesus had healed him. They could not have it!

The rejection of the blind man by the Jewish leaders prompted Jesus to use the metaphor of the Shepherd and His sheep. Jesus wanted to point out that He, the very One they were rejecting, is the only way into God's true sheepfold. And so He said that everyone else is a thief and a robber.

Let me urge you to read John 9:35 through John 10. List in your notebook everything you learn from John 10 about the Shepherd and the sheep. You will be blessed by what you see.

# 90

*J*esus said, "I am the good shepherd, and I know My own, and My own know Me" (John 10:14). Others may not recognize Jesus. They may say, as the Jews did, "You are a Samaritan and have a demon" (John 8:48). Or they may accuse Jesus of being "insane" (John 10:20); but that does not change who He is any more than it changes who you are when men reject and revile you and say all manner of evil against you falsely (Matthew 5:11).

Read the Word, Beloved, and you will know what God says about you. Then believe that, rather than the angry accusations of sinful men. Read the whole counsel of God—the Word in its entirety—and you will know the truth about Jesus Christ. Remember, John 8:32 says, "You will know the truth, and the truth will make you free."

It is Satan who is the father of lies. Many times Satan uses religious men as his tools in his effort to destroy the flock of God. The Jews were the ones who had the demon, so to speak. Because they were of their father, the devil, it followed that they would want to do the desires of their father.

No wonder they wanted to kill Jesus and rid themselves of those who followed Him! Yet in their very plot to kill Jesus, they would be part of the sovereign plan of God to sacrifice the Shepherd for the sake of His sheep. In this incredible metaphor in John 10, Jesus points out the Jews as mere hirelings who flee when the wolf comes because they are "not concerned about the sheep" (10:13). Their concern is their own profit! No, these Jews would not take Jesus' life until He, as the Good Shepherd, was ready to lay down His life for the sheep. And no matter what they said about Jesus, they were wrong. In John 10, we see Jesus as: a) the True Shepherd: the Door of God's sheep (10:1-9); b) the Good Shepherd: the One who lays down His life for the sheep (10:10-21); and c) the Father's Shepherd: the One to whom the Father gave the sheep (10:22-42).

John 10 begins with the words "truly, truly." The King James Version renders it "verily, verily." One of my black sisters told me they translate it "sho' nuff, sho' nuff," and that is exactly what "truly, truly" or "verily, verily" means. It means that what Jesus is saying is absolutely true, absolutely sure. You can stake your life on it.

According to John 10, there is only one way to get into the fold of the sheep, and that is through the Door. Jesus said, "Truly, truly, I say to you, I am the door of the sheep" (10:7). There is absolutely no other way to enter into eternal life for Jew or Gentile, Muslim, Catholic, or Protestant. Each may enter only through Jesus, the Shepherd of the sheep, the One who is one with the Father.

# 91

The Old Testament is filled with references to God as the Shepherd of His people Israel. Therefore, since Jesus is God incarnate, it is only logical that He would explain to the Jews that He is the true Shepherd of Israel and not only of Israel but of "other sheep, which are not of [Israel's] fold" (John 10:16). When a Jew heard Jesus say that He was "the good shepherd," immediately his mind would run to key Old Testament passages where the metaphor of the *shepherd* or *sheep* played a major role.

One of these passages is in Isaiah—that awesome book which speaks repeatedly of the coming of Messiah, of His titles and His kingdom. In Isaiah 53—a chapter now seldom read in many synagogues because it so accurately describes the redemptive ministry of Jesus Christ—we meet our proneness to wander: "All of us like sheep have gone astray, each of us has turned to his own way; but the Lord has caused the iniquity of us all to fall on Him" (53:6). Wouldn't the remembrance of this verse correlate with the fact that Jesus had just said He would lay down His life for the sheep?

Surely Jesus' reference to *shepherd* and *sheep* would cause them to recall the comforting words of Psalm 23:1: "The Lord is my shepherd, I shall not want." The Hebrew word for *Lord* was the most holy and awesome name of God, *YHWH*, first called *Yahweh* and then later called *Jehovah*. With the use of this name, they should have understood that if Jesus was their Shepherd, then Jesus is Jehovah—one with God! And if Jesus is our Shepherd, then He is the One who will provide all our needs, who will guide us all the days of our lives, and who will cause us to "dwell in the house of the LORD forever" (23:6).

Where the shepherds of Israel had failed to properly care for the flock of God, Jesus would not fail. Surely this would bring to the Jewish mind Ezekiel 34, where God tells of His distress with the shepherds of Israel, hirelings who cared more for themselves than for the flock of God. Thus, God said to Ezekiel, "Son of man, prophesy against the shepherds of Israel. Prophesy and say to those shepherds, 'Thus says the Lord GOD, "Woe, shepherds of Israel who have been feeding themselves! Should not the shepherds feed the flock?...My flock was scattered over all the surface of the earth, and there was no one to search or seek for them"'...'Behold, I Myself will search for My sheep and seek them out'" (34:2,6,11).

Ezekiel prophesied for God, and there God was in the Person of His Son, the true Shepherd, the Good Shepherd, the Father's Shepherd who came that His sheep might have life and have it more abundantly. What did it matter that they had cast out the blind man? Jesus gave him sight and took him into God's fold!

# 92

*I*f any animal ever needed a shepherd to care for it, it is a sheep. I believe God made sheep helpless to give us a picture of our desperate need of Him as the Shepherd of our life.

The book that has been most helpful to me in this study is Phillip Keller's *A Shepherd Looks at Psalm 23*. It would be excellent to use in your family devotions. I want to share with you some wonderful insights on sheep. As you read, keep reminding yourself that you are His sheep.

Sheep need constant care and guidance. Their welfare depends solely upon the care they receive from their shepherd. So the more attentive the shepherd, the better cared for are the sheep. When you see sheep that are weak, sickly, and infested with pests, you can be sure their shepherd does not tend them well. It is possible too that they have been left to the care of hirelings who do not feel personally responsible.

Psalm 23:1 says, "The LORD is my shepherd, I shall not want." Obviously, if the sheep doesn't want, his shepherd is attending him well. The remainder of Psalm 23 recounts the ways in which the Shepherd meets the needs of His sheep. You will find the information I am about to give you far more exciting if you read Psalm 23 before you go any further.

We know the Christian's life is to be one of rest—the rest of faith. If we are weary and heavy-laden, Jesus bids us come to Him that He might give us rest (Matthew 11:28). Sheep need rest, but they cannot lie down in green pastures unless they are free from four things. We will consider these next time. Today, thank your Shepherd for His constant attention to your every concern.

# 23

*I*f the sheep are going to rest, they must be free from flies, parasites, and other pests that would affect their health and make them restless. They must also be free from hunger. If not fed properly, sheep will be moving about constantly, foraging for food. And in their foraging, they are apt to wander and fall prey to wolves. This is why God constantly reminds His undershepherds to feed His flock. And this is why, my beloved friend, I write books and other study material.

Another factor that will hinder sheep from lying down in green pastures is fear. They must sense no danger from without. Because sheep are helpless, timid, and feeble, they easily fall prey to other animals. When they encounter another animal, they will often stop dead in their tracks and freeze, rather than running for safety or crying out. Without their shepherd, they are totally defenseless.

If sheep are going to rest, they must also be free from tension. If other sheep are tormenting them, they do not lie down in peace, but stay on their feet continuously.

Have you ever been or are you being tormented by those in the body who are not tender and caring, who do not love you unconditionally? When you are sick and hurting, lean and weak, does it seem they come to your destruction rather than your aid? Have you ever been shoved about by the strong and been wounded as they pushed you aside in your weakened state?

O Beloved, if you understand what I am saying, then I urge you not to do the same to another! In 1 Thessalonians, Paul urges the brethren, "Admonish the unruly, encourage the fainthearted, help the weak, be patient with everyone. See that no one repays another with evil for evil, but always seek after that which is good for one another and for all people" (5:14,15).

When there is sin in the camp, it must be dealt with so that the sinning one is brought to repentance. However, this process should always be entered into as the Shepherd of sheep would do it—in love governed by a desire for the highest good of another.

In Ezekiel 34, God was upset not only with the shepherds of Israel, but also the fat and strong sheep who did not care for the lean and weak. For when they are not cared for, in their restlessness they scatter. Thus, God Himself searches for His scattered sheep, seeks them out, and leads them to rest: "I will seek the lost, bring back the scattered, bind up the broken and strengthen the sick; but the fat and the strong I will destroy. I will feed them with judgment....I will judge between one sheep and another, between the rams and the male goats...between the fat sheep and the lean sheep. Because you push with side and with shoulder, and thrust at all the weak with your horns until you have scattered them abroad, therefore, I will deliver My flock" (34:16-22).

What lessons our Shepherd has for us as His sheep! May we learn them well so we don't have to be judged by Him.

# 94

$S$heep are creatures of habit. If they are left to themselves, they will graze the same ground over and over again, walking the same trails until the land becomes wasteland, eroded with gullies from the path worn by the sheep. Ground overgrazed by sheep often becomes polluted with parasites and disease. Thus, God writes through Ezekiel: "Is it too slight a thing for you that you should feed in the good pasture, that you must tread down with your feet the rest of your pastures? Or that you should drink of the clear waters, that you must foul the rest with your feet? As for My flock, they must eat what you tread down with your feet and drink what you foul with your feet!" (34:18,19).

I believe God was irate with the fat and strong sheep, because they were fouling up and polluting the Word of God with their false prophecies, their visions and dreams. They had the Word of God, but they were not giving it to the people. Jeremiah, a contemporary of Ezekiel, said to the prophets, "For you will no longer remember the oracle of the LORD, because every man's own word will become the oracle, and you have perverted the words of the living God, the LORD of hosts, our God" (Jeremiah 23:36).

If sheep are not led to proper pastures, they will eat or drink things that are harmful to them. Therefore, many times the shepherd goes before them and prepares a table for their grazing. The "table" will be carefully searched for any plants that could poison the sheep. Thus in Psalm 23:5, we read of the Lord, our Shepherd, preparing a table for us in the presence of our enemies. The Shepherd's concern is that His sheep be properly nourished.

Sheep cannot live without water, and yet they can go for months without actually drinking water, if the weather is not too hot. Sheep get their water from three sources: streams or springs, deep wells, or the dew on the grass. The morning dew can carry them until their grazing takes them to streams, springs, or wells. The secret is for the sheep to eat the grass while it is still wet with dew. It is that day-by-day grazing on grass laden with morning dew that sustains them during the heat of the day.

O what a lesson for us as the sheep of His pasture! Grazing in the morning, so we can withstand the heat of the day! Remember what Jesus said: "If anyone is thirsty, let him come to Me and drink." Are you drinking the dew, dear one?

# 95

The condition of the sheep reflects the love and the care of the shepherd—or the lack of it. God has always been the true Shepherd of His sheep, and yet He has appointed under Him earthly shepherds to watch over His flock. He is the Chief Shepherd; they are undershepherds.

We see this both in the Old and New Testaments. In 1 Peter 5:2-4, we find an admonition to the elders: "Shepherd the flock of God among you, exercising oversight not under compulsion, but voluntarily, according to the will of God; and not for sordid gain, but with eagerness; nor yet as lording it over those allotted to your charge, but proving to be examples to the flock. And when the Chief Shepherd appears, you will receive the unfading crown of glory."

In this passage, you see the concern of the Father that the shepherd lay down his life for the sheep, rather than shepherding them for personal gain. As you read John 10, you can't miss Jesus' repeated statement that He was going to lay down His life for the sheep. Over and over again, God stresses the fact that the primary concern of the shepherd is to be the welfare of his sheep. O what a difference it would make in Christendom if each leader, each undershepherd, understood that the condition of his flock was a reflection of his love and care for his sheep!

In the verses from 1 Peter, you saw that the shepherd is not to lord it over his sheep. There is to be only one lord in Christendom, and that is the Lord Jesus Christ. No person is to have preeminence. And any man or woman who is a true follower of Jesus will follow His example: "For even the Son of Man did not come to be served, but to serve, and to give His life a ransom for many" (Mark 10:45).

In John 10, as in Ezekiel 34, you see the vivid contrast between the Jews' and Jesus' shepherding of God's flock. The Jewish leaders used the sheep for their benefit rather than seeing that they existed for the benefit of the sheep.

O Beloved, I do not know what responsibilities the Lord has given you in His kingdom; even if He has given you only one little sheep to tend, remember that the condition of that sheep reflects on your shepherding.

Why don't you take a few minutes to meditate upon your lifestyle. How does it compare to the high calling of your Shepherd? How are you living as His sheep? Are you sure that you are in His fold, that you have entered in by Him, the only Door to the Father?

# 96

*W*hen a shepherd would bring his flocks from the fields into a nearby village, he would often leave them in a sheepfold for the night. There they would file into a lean-to erected against the wall of a building, and join sheep from other flocks.

You might wonder how the shepherd would sort his sheep from the others, since they all look so much alike. You might think they needed a distinctive mark.

However, sorting out sheep by identifying their marks is not necessary for a true shepherd. His sheep know his voice. When he calls them, they respond.

When Jesus spoke of the sheep and the Shepherd to the Pharisees, He was telling them why the blind man had seen and believed, and also why they had become blind. They were blind because they were not His sheep. If they belonged to Him, they would hear His voice and follow Him. He wanted to show them there was only one way into God's fold—through the door. He did not want them to miss the fact that He was the Door.

Sheep recognize the voice of their shepherd. Another may try to imitate the shepherd's call, and may even use the same names for the sheep the shepherd uses, but it won't entice them. The sheep know the voice of their shepherd! Therefore, when the shepherd comes to the sheepfold to claim his sheep, "To him the doorkeeper opens, and the sheep hear his voice, and he calls his own sheep by name and leads them out. When he puts forth all his own, he goes before them, and the sheep follow him because they know his voice. A stranger they simply will not follow, but will flee from him, because they do not know the voice of strangers" (John 10:3-5).

O little sheep, doesn't it absolutely thrill your heart to know that you were His before the foundation of the world? When you heard His Word, His voice, you knew at last you had found your Shepherd. Hallelujah!

# 97

*T*hose who came before Jesus, claiming to be Messiah and to know the way to life eternal, were thieves and robbers. They wanted to use the sheep for their own selfish purposes. They were coming "to steal and kill and destroy" (John 10:10), just like the one they represented, their father, the devil. But "the sheep did not hear them." They fled, knowing that their voice was not the voice of the true Shepherd (John 10:5).

God has given me the great joy of hearing testimonies of many people who in their search to know God went from one religion to another but were never satisfied, until finally they met Jesus. They discovered that He was the Door! Once they entered in through Him, they were saved and went "in and out" and found pasture (John 10:9).

When people are truly born again because they hear the voice of the Shepherd and in faith believe the truth of the Word of God, then they enter through the Door and find perfect security. They are home at last, a part of God's flock, His forever family. Now they walk in perfect liberty, for they "will go in and out," and finding pasture, they have perfect sustenance (John 10:9). Finding the truth and feasting on the truth, God's Word, they are now able to rest.

And what shall be the end of these sheep? The beginning! The beginning of life eternal. Jesus said, "My sheep hear My voice, and I know them, and they follow Me; and I give eternal life to them, and they will never perish; and no one will snatch them out of My hand.

My Father, who has given them to Me, is greater than all; and no one is able to snatch them out of the Father's hand" (John 10:27-29).

Once again, Jesus is reminding those who do not believe that the reason for their unbelief is because they were not given by the Father to the Son. He said, "You do not believe because you are not of My sheep" (John 10:26).

Throughout the Gospel of John we have seen man's responsibility to believe and be born again. But we have also seen that our birth into His family is by the will of God. This is the Godward aspect of salvation which doesn't contradict or make void the human aspect. The Word teaches both. Accept both in faith.

## 98

*D*o you struggle with seemingly contradictory Scriptures? Some show, on the one hand, the responsibility of man in believing on the Lord Jesus Christ; and others, on the other hand, say that we are given to the Son by the Father, chosen by Him before the foundation of the world. Don't try to rationalize them so that you distort their meaning. Instead allow the Scriptures to speak for themselves.

Faith doesn't need to reason and say, "But if God chooses and gives, then man is not responsible; he is a mere robot!" Faith merely bows the knee and says, "Father, whether I can reconcile the sovereignty of God and the free will of man in relation to salvation is not important. I recognize that Your ways are not my ways and that Your thoughts are not my thoughts. Yours are so much higher than mine. Therefore, I will simply take You at Your Word. I will not carry any doctrine to any extreme to which You do not carry it. I will simply believe what You say and allow You to speak for Yourself."

Now then, Beloved, having said all that, let's return to John 10. You must understand this passage in its context. Remember that John wrote so his readers might know of the signs Jesus performed which showed Him to be the Christ, the Son of God. These were written that we might believe and in believing might have life in His name (John 20:30,31).

But what about those who saw the signs and did not believe? Why did some believe and others did not? Why did the religious leaders for the most part not believe? And why did they try to take away Jesus' life? Let's take these questions one by one, for the answers are all in John 10.

The Jewish leaders for the most part did not believe because they were not of God's sheep. "The Jews then gathered around Him, and were saying to Him, 'How long will You keep us in suspense? If You are the Christ, tell us plainly.' Jesus answered them, 'I told you, and you do not believe; the works that I do in My Father's name, these testify of Me. But you do not believe because you are not of My sheep'" (10:24-26).

God is the Author, the Initiator of our salvation: They saw the signs but did not believe. Let me remind you again of what Jesus said to the multitude who followed Him because of the loaves and fish. He told them that we are given by the Father to the Son, drawn to Him by the Father; and as we hear and learn from the Father, we come to Jesus (John 6:37,39,44,45).

O Sheep, this is for your comfort. Accept it and rest in the character of your God.

## 99

*I*f you can accept the sovereignty of God in your salvation as taught in the Word of God, it will bring you great peace in dealing with the death of your loved ones. So often I have watched people agonize over the death of another because they were not sure whether the person really knew the Lord Jesus Christ. And in their agony, they would begin to torment themselves with "if onlys": "If only I had been a better witness." "If only I had gone to see her and had shared the gospel one more time." "If only he hadn't died so suddenly. Maybe if he had lived longer, he would have been saved." To live with these "if onlys" is not only agony, it is needless. No "if only" would have saved them if they had not already been saved.

This reality is the blessed comfort of understanding the teaching our Lord gives to us in John 6 and 10. Those who are truly His sheep cannot die without hearing the voice of the Shepherd. His sheep *will* hear His voice.

When speaking to the Jews, Jesus said, "I have other sheep, which are not of this fold; I *must* bring them also, and they *will* hear My voice; and they *will become* one flock with one shepherd" (John 10:16, emphasis added). Of all that the Father has given Jesus, He will "lose nothing, but raise it up on the last day" (John 6:39). A person who has been given to the Son by the Father cannot die until he believes on the Lord Jesus Christ. And if a person dies without receiving the Lord Jesus

Christ, then he never would have believed even if he had lived for hundreds of years.

God does not lose His sheep. They hear His voice, He gives them eternal life, and they shall never perish. This, Beloved, is the comfort of understanding the Godward aspect of salvation. God is in control of life and death.

Deuteronomy 32:39 says, "See now that I, I am He, and there is no god besides Me; it is I who put to death and give life....There is no one who can deliver from My hand." Jesus has "the keys of death and of Hades" (Revelation 1:18).

Jesus confronted the religious leaders who were plotting to put Him to death with this truth. They had no power to take His life from Him. In one mighty breath Jesus addressed the disregard these leaders showed for their sheep and also confronted their impotence to take His life: "For this reason the Father loves Me, because I lay down My life so that I may take it again. No one has taken it away from Me, but I lay it down on My own initiative. I have authority to lay it down, and I have authority to take it up again" (John 10:17,18). These leaders were not willing to lay down their lives for the sheep. They had just put one out, because he believed on Jesus when He touched his physical blindness. But Jesus had taken him in. He was one of God's sheep.

Do you wonder if you are? O Beloved, the very desire to be His sheep is because you are—or because you are in the process of becoming one.

# *100*

*R*emember I said that if you were going to be saved, you couldn't die before salvation? Let me share the content of two letters, one from a Precept student, Joyce, and the other from her Precept leader. I shed tears of joy when I read these as I thought, "Father, this is what life and ministry are all about...people coming to know You and Your Word! O thank You for these women who are reaching out to others."

Both letters centered around the same person: a 74-year-old woman.

Dear Kay,

I must share my experience with you. I am taking the Genesis II course. Several Fridays ago in early January, my friend Susie visited our Precept study with me. We were nearing the end of the Genesis course. Susie became so excited that she ordered the In & Out for Genesis II.

Susie is a registered nurse. She is now 74, so she doesn't nurse but she is active. She is married to a physician who was stricken with a massive stroke and is confined to a nursing home with only the use of his right arm and hand. Susie was a constant visitor to her husband at the nursing home.

I had worked for her husband for 29 years, and during those years, Susie and I had become close friends. But during the last several years, we had drifted apart. I was so thrilled with this new Precept Bible study I had to share this with her, but at first, Susie found many excuses why she could not attend. After her first visit, that changed.

At this point, let me share the Precept leader's insight:

As Joyce mentioned, she and Susie have been close friends for many years, but lately they had seen less of each other. Joyce was so overjoyed when Susie finally decided to attend our Bible study. As Susie heard us share what we had learned, and listened as you taught on tape, I could see the knowledge and joy of the Lord bring a glow to her face.

I think one of the outstanding benefits of being a Precept leader is being able to watch the expressions change as people grasp a new truth of God's Word and how it relates to them. Susie was very enthusiastic about getting into the Genesis II study.

The story will be continued tomorrow, but let me give you something to think about. Are you reaching out to others? Sharing your faith? You may want to get Joe Aldrich's book, *Life-Style Evangelism*. It will show you how you can in a very natural way.

## *101*

*B*ack to Joyce's letter:

> On Friday, January 23, Susie and I attended class.
> After class, one of the ladies asked Susie if she had ever
> given her life to Christ. She said excitedly, "Yes, I went
> forward when I was only 11 years old, and I remember
> that day."

The Precept leader then shared this: "As another member of the
class and I talked with Joyce and Susie after class about being born
again and how Susie could be sure if she was, I suggested Susie read
1 John and especially note the phrases such as: 'We know that we have
come to know Him if…'"

Back now to the student's letter:

> I drove Susie home, and she asked me about the
> Trinity. Then she said she loved the calm directness of
> our leader. As we talked, she shared that she wondered
> if she would be able to have enough strength for the
> things that would be facing her in days to come. I told
> her she would have strength given to her beyond human
> understanding. Little did I know!

Then Friday evening, I phoned her and asked her if she had listened to your testimony tape. She was so excited and exclaimed she was just going to phone me. She said she had listened to the first side, and then she said, "I must be born again. Next Friday I want to stay after class and talk with our leader, and I want to again verbally give my life to Christ before people. I want to have you come up with me and hold my hand."

On Sunday afternoon, January 25, 1987, Susie was visiting her husband at the nursing home when she had a massive coronary and dropped dead.

Before the next Friday class, Susie was buried. When we met the following Friday, we all felt God had personally touched our lives.

Our friend and classmate had left this world. Buried Thursday, January 29.

In the casket, by her head, was a card placed there by her family. They found the note on the wall of her kitchen, near her opened Bible. The note read:

> *God is my Father; Jesus is my personal Savior;*
> *the Holy Spirit lives within me. If God is for us,*
> *who can be against us?*

Her daughters said she called each of them that Friday night and was so happy. His sheep had heard His voice, and He had given her eternal life.

# 102

Our Lord's words bring division. This often makes delivering the gospel a difficult assignment, because we want to be accepted, approved. We don't like to be laughed at, ridiculed, rejected. Yet many times living for Jesus Christ results in this treatment. A popular gospel which can be accepted by all is not the true gospel. The way to heaven is narrow, "the gate is small," and few there are who enter in (Matthew 7:13,14).

How well our Lord reminded us: "Woe to you when all men speak well of you" (Luke 6:26). If they did not speak well of our Lord, should they speak well of us? Of course not! "A slave is not greater than his master" (John 13:16).

As I say all this, I am not excusing people who are rude and ungracious in their delivery of the gospel. It is His words that are to convict and, thus, sometimes bring offense. Our behavior or manner in delivering His gospel should never offend.

Although He hated the sin, Jesus always loved the sinner. Thus, you find Him eating with publicans and sinners, coming not to condemn those who were already condemned but offering them life. However, life was not offered on their terms but on His. It is at this point that the gospel brings offense. It can never be compromised.

Salvation is always on God's terms. When the gospel is presented on those terms, we can be sure His sheep will hear His voice. However, those who are not His often will turn and revile not only the gospel but also those who deliver it.

We see this in John 10:19: "A division occurred again among the Jews because of these words." This is not the first mention of a division in the Gospel of John. In John 7:43, we read: "So a division occurred in the crowd because of Him." And again in John 9:16, we read of how the words of Jesus divide: "Therefore some of the Pharisees were saying, 'This man is not from God, because He does not keep the Sabbath.' But others were saying, 'How can a man who is a sinner perform such signs?' And there was a division among them."

In each of these incidents, the division existed among religious people. Of course, there will be a division with the world because men prefer darkness rather than light. But you expect that response of the world.

When Jesus' words cause division among those who profess to be His followers, it is hard. A division is usually created by those who call Him "Lord, Lord" but who do not do the things He commands them. The division may result too from those who have a form of godliness but know nothing of the power of God. They know about God, but have never entered into a relationship with Him. They have a "self-righteousness" that has not submitted to His righteousness. Therefore, His words bring division.

# *103*

Standing on the Washington shoreline of the Pacific Ocean, he lifted his head toward heaven, gazed at the billows of clouds, and addressed the God who dwelt far beyond them. He was confident that if God was there He could hear his challenge: "God, if You really exist, if Jesus is really Your Son, then let me walk on water like Jesus let Peter do." Frank wanted to know if God existed, but he wanted to know on his terms. So with gauntlet thrown to the ground, he stepped into the water, not onto the water! He waded up to his knees and then turned back. He was adamantly convinced there was no God. He lived with his conviction until, as an old man in his seventies, unable to speak and dying of cancer, he finally took God at His Word and gave in to Jesus. A day later Frank entered into the presence of the God who had not enabled him to walk on water just to prove Himself God.

People have not changed. Like the Jews, Frank pressured Jesus for more evidence of who He was. At the time of the Feast of Dedication, "Jesus was walking in the temple in the portico of Solomon. The Jews then gathered around Him, and were saying to Him, 'How long will You keep us in suspense? If You are the Christ, tell us plainly.' Jesus answered them, 'I told you, and you do not believe; the works that I do in My Father's name, these testify of Me'" (John 10:23-25).

Frank wanted a new work, a repeat of a miracle God had performed when Peter walked on water. The Jews had seen many signs. They had heard from Jesus' own lips that He was the Son of God, the I AM, one with the Father. But they would not believe. They understood very clearly that Jesus claimed to be God (John 10:33), but still they would not believe.

How plain does Jesus have to be? How plain does God have to be? God has supernaturally superintended the writing of His Word. He has watched over it and kept it from error in the original manuscripts and preserved it down through the centuries. He has given us evidence after evidence in history and archaeology of the veracity of His Word. Yet we want Him to let us walk on water!

Enough, Beloved! You have enough evidence. You have a record of His works done in the presence of many witnesses—miracles which no man could do apart from God. And you have a record of His words—words which are spirit and life. Now you must take God at His word. Faith comes just as it did to Frank, through the hearing of God's Word. Your part is to believe.

# 104

Sometime after the winter of the Feast of Dedication and before the Passover, Jesus went to stay beyond the Jordan, where John the Baptist had done his baptizing. It was during this time that Lazarus, Jesus' friend, became ill. His sisters Mary and Martha sent a message from Bethany to inform Jesus of Lazarus' illness. Whether they suspected that Lazarus would have died or not, we do not know.

However, there is one thing we know for sure. Mary and Martha were well aware of the Lord's healing ministry. And there is no record in the Scriptures of anyone ever dying in the presence of our Lord. From what they both said to Jesus after Lazarus' death, I am sure they believed that should death have come lurking in the shadows of their brother's room, it could not have dared touch him in the presence of the Son of God!

Yet, Jesus did not go to Bethany when He received the message of Lazarus' illness. Lazarus died and Jesus came later. When He arrived, both Mary and Martha were convinced that if only Jesus had come, Lazarus "would not have died" (John 11:21,32).

For the remainder of this study, I want us to look at and meditate on some invaluable truths from John 11 that will enable you to handle death better when you meet it face-to-face either in your own life or in the life of a loved one. Often even Christians are ill-prepared to confront and deal with death. It seems to be an enemy, an unwelcome intruder. We may feel that if we don't consider it, then it cannot happen.

How wrong we are! Unless Jesus returns, we will all see death. When death grasped Caesar Brogia by the hand, he cried, "When I lived, I provided for everything but death; now I must die, and I am unprovided to die!"

When Dr. Charles Weigle, the composer of the song "No One Ever Cared for Me Like Jesus," died, he was in a hospital room in Chattanooga, Tennessee. A nurse, walking by his room, saw him sitting up in bed with his arms stretched toward the ceiling. Stepping into his room, she said cheerfully, "Are you all right, Dr. Weigle?" "O Nurse, I'm going home. I'm going home." Touched by the sweetness of her frail patient, she went to his bed, patted his arm, and replied tenderly, "No, Dr. Weigle, you can't go home. You're too sick." But he looked at her, arms still raised: "No, I am going home." And he went home straight into the arms of the One who had cared for him.

Read John 11, asking God to remove any fears or misconceptions of death that would bind you.

# 105

*H*ave you ever wondered how love could allow suffering and death? Have you ever thought that if you were God, you certainly would put an end to evil, to war, to suffering, to death? If you have, you are not alone. Those thoughts are common to man.

Evil, war, suffering, and death are hard to experience, but God permits them because they serve His purposes. Remember that His purposes are far beyond our comprehension because our understanding is finite. So God bids us "walk by faith, not by sight" (2 Corinthians 5:7). He calls us to "look not at the things which are seen, but at the things which are not seen" (2 Corinthians 4:18). He instructs us to give thanks in all things (1 Thessalonians 5:18). He comforts us with the knowledge that all things will "work together for good to those who love God, to those who are called according to His purpose" (Romans 8:28).

As we look at John 11, I want to share eight truths which will loosen death's grave clothes. In the loosening you will be set free from the fear of death and from the sorrow which has no hope.

The first truth is: *Love allows suffering and death.* When Mary and Martha sent a message to tell Jesus of Lazarus' illness, they were convinced that He would come immediately. They knew Jesus loved them. They knew too He was able to heal the sick. And so they sent a message to Him saying, "Lord, behold, he whom You love is sick" (John 11:3).

Can you imagine what it must have been like to wait for His arrival? I wonder how many times they went to the door to look for the One who could alleviate their pain and distress. Watching Lazarus' weakened condition as he fought for life, they wondered if the Lord would come in time.

Years ago I sat with my mother at the bedside of my father in the intensive care unit of the Venice Hospital, waiting for God to heal my father. He had undergone five major surgeries in 12 days. Before they amputated his leg, I looked at his almost-black foot and prayed, "O Father, I know, if You want to, You can speak a word and bring back the circulation to my father's leg." I knew God could—I didn't lack faith—but God didn't choose to heal my father's leg or the rest of his body.

On April 22, 1980, the days God had ordained for my father came to an end. My precious, precious daddy died. And in the process, God allowed him and us—to suffer. Did God love him or us any less? Was God any less who He is for allowing this heartache?

No! Love has been and always will be one of the attributes of God. Love allows suffering and death.

# *106*

$W$hen love delays, when God does not answer your prayers the way you think He should, you can know, precious child of God, He is in the process of building your faith. And in the building of your faith, others will be reached and ministered to. This brings us to the second truth that will loosen death's grave clothes which would incapacitate you and keep you from serving God. This freeing truth is: *For the Christian, suffering and death are platforms for faith.*

Faith is not faith until it is tested, and what could test it more than suffering or death? The way you and I respond in suffering can either contradict the words of our profession or it can bring glory to God.

In John 11:4, we hear Jesus say, "This sickness is not to end in death, but for the glory of God, so that the Son of God may be glorified by it." To which you may reply, "Yes, God was glorified because Lazarus was raised from the dead, but my loved one died! Can that glorify God?" It can, Beloved, if you will walk in the promise and assurance of who Jesus is, if you will hold fast in faith to the truth that He is "the resurrection and the life." For the one who believes in Him "will live even if he dies" (John 11:25). God will be glorified if you will not allow yourself to grieve as those "who have no hope" (1 Thessalonians 4:13).

Jesus said to Martha, "Everyone who lives and believes in Me will never die"; and then He asked her, "Do you believe this?" (John 11:26). He will ask you the same thing when you face death, either your own or that of a loved one. How you answer that question, how you respond to death, will display your faith.

O Beloved, may you and I learn it well: In every trial, every testing, every temptation, we can live out the sufficiency of His grace and the reality of our faith. Everyone wants a story with a happy ending. We hope for a future, not disaster. We long for success, not defeat. We love to hear of those who overcome.

And this, child of God, is our inheritance in Christ Jesus. Every occasion of suffering and death can have a happy ending if we will cling in faith to the blessed hope of the resurrection and the life, where God "will wipe away every tear from their eyes; and there will no longer be any death; there will no longer be any mourning, or crying, or pain," for "the first things" will "have passed away" (Revelation 21:4).

According to John 11:15, Lazarus was allowed to die that others might believe. May you and I see that whatever God permits has a purpose. May we not miss His purpose, but see it as a platform for faith.

# *107*

The fear of death is an incredibly powerful weapon that Satan wields through human agency, and evil men have always sought to intimidate and rule others through this fear. Yet to the Christian, death should be but a rubber sword. When Jesus decided to go back to Judea, to Mary and Martha in Bethany, "the disciples said to Him, 'Rabbi, the Jews were just now seeking to stone You, and are You going there again?' Jesus answered, 'Are there not twelve hours in the day? If anyone walks in the day, he does not stumble, because he sees the light of this world. But if anyone walks in the night, he stumbles, because the light is not in him'" (John 11:8-10).

The Son of Man did not fear death but rested in the sovereignty of God. The Jews could not kill Him until God was ready. When they did crucify Him, it served God's purpose.

Deuteronomy 32:39 assures us that God kills and makes alive. None is greater than God, and none can take our lives without His permission. Satan ruled man through fear of death. The devil at one time had the power of death because of man's sin. At Calvary, Jesus paid the wages of sin—which was death—so that Satan no longer rules over us through sin. "Since the children share in flesh and blood, He Himself likewise also partook of the same, that through death He might render powerless him who had the power of death, that is, the devil, and might free those who through fear of death were subject to slavery all their lives" (Hebrews 2:14,15).

Because we are freed from sin, "death no longer is master" over us (Romans 6:9). Hallelujah! Jesus holds "the keys of death and of Hades" (Revelation 1:18).

# *108*

$W$e come now to the third truth that will loosen death's fear-binding grave clothes: *Following the Light of the world will keep you from stumbling over the fear of death.*

Let me ask you mothers and fathers a question: Would you keep your children home from some mission field of service for fear they might lose their lives? Or for fear that you might not see them again before you die?

To let the fear of death rule you is to walk in darkness rather than in the light. When you walk in darkness, you stumble. To digress from God's purpose, through fear of death or for any other reason, is to walk in darkness. God forbid that you or I should stumble through life, or that we should cause our loved ones to stumble, because we do not believe our God and walk in obedience to His Word. If Jesus had listened to well-meaning people, you and I would not have a Savior.

You need to take a few minutes, Beloved, and meditate upon these truths. Ask God to show you if fear is ruling your life. Wait before Him and write out anything He shows you. Then in faith, put it away. Remember, your times are in His hands—hands pierced by love. Thank Him that His perfect love casts out fear (1 John 4:18).

# *109*

*T*o the Christian, death is not final. A believer simply falls asleep in Jesus and wakes up instantly in the presence of God. If anything ought to loosen death's grave clothes, it is this fourth truth: *For the Christian, death is but falling asleep in Jesus.*

Jesus said to the disciples, "'Our friend Lazarus has fallen asleep; but I go, so that I may awaken him out of sleep.' The disciples then said to Him, 'Lord, if he has fallen asleep, he will recover.' Now Jesus had spoken of his death; but they thought that He was speaking of literal sleep. So Jesus then said to them plainly, 'Lazarus is dead'" (John 11:11-14).

As you study what the Scriptures say regarding death and the Christian, it is obvious that death is drastically different for the lost and the saved. For the lost, death is never to experience life. It is to lose any opportunity to ever believe on the Lord Jesus Christ, for "there is salvation in no one else; for there is no other name under heaven that has been given among men by which we must be saved" (Acts 4:12). Therefore, those who do not believe on the Lord Jesus Christ in this life will perish, for "it is appointed for men to die once and after this comes judgment" (Hebrews 9:27).

Those who die without the Lord Jesus Christ are referred to as "the dead." Someday the dead will stand before the Great White Throne of God and be judged according to the things which were written in the books, according to their deeds. They will then be cast into the lake of fire. "This is the second death, the lake of fire. And if anyone's name was not found written in the book of life, he was thrown into the lake of fire" (Revelation 20:14,15).

What a contrast with those who have received the Lord Jesus Christ! Job wrote: "As for me, I know that my Redeemer lives, and at the last He will take His stand on the earth. Even after my skin is destroyed, yet from my flesh I shall see God; whom I myself shall behold, and whom my eyes will see and not another" (Job 19:25-27).

Some say that when Christians die, they sleep in the grave until Jesus returns and raises the dead. However, Paul said, "To live is Christ and to die is gain" (Philippians 1:21). To sleep in the grave would not be gain! Paul knew that physical death would allow him to "depart and be with Christ," which, he said, "is very much better" (Philippians 1:23).

When Paul talks about putting off our earthly tent, he says to be "absent from the body" is "to be at home with the Lord" (2 Corinthians 5:1-9). In 1 Thessalonians 4:13-18, he refers to those who have died in Christ as having "fallen asleep in Jesus" because this is what death is to the believer—falling asleep and waking up in the presence of our Lord. Rejoice, O child of God!

# *110*

$T$he very minute you believe on the Lord Jesus Christ you pass from death to life. You will never experience death as the unbeliever does. Your spirit simply leaves your earthly body and goes immediately into the presence of God the Father, the Son, and the Holy Spirit. And at the moment of your entrance into heaven, you will join your loved ones who have preceded you. You will recognize them, even as Moses and Elijah were recognized at the transfiguration of Jesus.

Thus, we come to the fifth truth from John 11 which will loosen death's grave clothes: *Because Jesus is the Resurrection and the Life, the Christian will not see death.* This truth caused Jesus to proclaim, "I am the resurrection and the life; he who believes in Me will live even if he dies, and everyone who lives and believes in Me will never die" (11:25,26).

When Jesus says those who believe in Him will never die, it is obvious that He does not mean we will never leave this body through what we call physical death. Rather, I believe He is saying we will never experience death as an unbeliever does.

Why? Because in His death, burial, and resurrection, Jesus "abolished death and brought life and immortality to light through the gospel" (2 Timothy 1:10). And since our Lord Jesus Christ resides within each believer (Colossians 1:27), we have eternal life within. "God has given us eternal life, and this life is in His Son. He who has the Son has the life; he who does not have the Son of God does not have the life" (1 John 5:11,12). How can one who has His life within ever die?

When my friends Bill and Ramona lost their 17-year-old Bryan in an automobile accident many years ago, they had never experienced such heart-wrenching pain. Yet Ramona wrote:

> Our Bryan met Jesus face to face in all His glory. What a glorious day for Bryan. But what a difficult day for our family. For Bryan, it was what he had been preparing for. God looked at Bryan and said, "Well done. Come on in. I have a place prepared just for you." I had read John 11:25,26 many times: "I am the resurrection and the life…everyone who…believes in Me shall never die.…" But the last four words in verse 26 hit me like a ton of bricks: "Do you believe this?"! I knew I had to answer that question. And once I said to the Lord, "Yes, I do believe," God began to show me His other promises. On the day Bryan died, I could either reject God or cling to Him. The choice was mine. Bill and I chose to cling to God. Our hurt was healed by believing His Word.

O Beloved, when you confront death, remember you will not see death. You'll see Jesus face-to-face!

## *III*

*J*esus wept." It is the shortest verse in the Bible and yet one of the most poignant. Although Jesus knew He was going to raise Lazarus from the dead, and that their sorrow would then be turned to joy, He still wept. He knows our pain and understands our sorrow, and He weeps because we weep.

With this, Beloved, we come to the sixth truth: *Because of God's sovereignty over death, the believer weeps but does not wail.* We can weep because the separation of death brings hurt, but we are not to wail, because we have hope. In 1 Thessalonians 4:13, Paul writes, "But we do not want you to be uninformed, brethren, about those who are asleep, so that you will not grieve as do the rest who have no hope." We grieve because death causes separation, loss, and loneliness; but we do not grieve as those who have no hope.

Someday the separation will be over, loss will be gain, and loneliness will be great rejoicing, for we shall all be with the Lord and with one another forever and ever (1 Thessalonians 4:16,17). All of this is ours, Beloved, because God is sovereign. He rules even over death. He is the Alpha and the Omega, the Beginning and the End (Revelation 22:13). "From Him and through Him and to Him are all things." Because we belong to Him, all things are ours as heirs of God and joint-heirs with Christ (Romans 11:36; 8:17).

So weep—Jesus wept. But do not wail. Wailing shows despair, and in Jesus, there is hope.

# *112*

$\mathcal{R}$amona and Bill had hope because they had seen the change in Bryan's life and because they believed God's Word. Bill shared:

> On Sunday night before his accident on the following Saturday, Bryan was asked by our Minister of Youth to share his testimony. Bryan loved the Lord very much and was a loving and caring young man. He never gave his mother and me any trouble during his 17 years with us. Bryan made a comment to our church that Sunday night: "I am excited about what the Lord is doing, and I feel that He is about to do something very special in my life." Bryan then read Philippians 1:6: "For I am confident of this very thing, that He who began a good work in you will perfect it until the day of Christ Jesus."
>
> On Saturday March 29, Bryan was killed instantly in a car accident on his way to the beach the last day of spring break. He was going only 15 to 20 MPH but hit a slick oil spot. My first reaction was one of disbelief. The next few days and weeks were filled with many feelings and emotions. I was mad at God for letting our son be killed. Then I came to realize that God never makes

a mistake; and even though I did not like or understand what had happened, I knew God still loved us and that Bryan was being cared for in heaven.

Bill and Ramona wept, but they did not wail. They rested in God's sovereignty.

# *113*

**D**eath was not God's desire. It came because of sin. Therefore, death has always been an enemy. When Jesus came face-to-face with death at the tomb of Lazarus, His indignation was so great that He was deeply moved in spirit (John 11:33) and snorted like a horse. This is what the term "deeply moved in spirit" means.[16] At that moment, Jesus, who came to conquer sin and death, confronted an enemy. We come now to our seventh truth: *Death is not an impossible, impassable barrier but a call to battle.*

Death came because of man's sin. God intended fellowship with man, not separation by death. I believe this is why Jesus wept at the tomb of Lazarus. There are three accounts in the Gospels of Jesus weeping, and all of them relate in one way or another to death. Let's look at them.

> When He [Jesus] approached Jerusalem, He saw the city and wept over it, saying, "If you had known in this day, even you, the things which make for peace! But now they have been hidden from your eyes. For the days will come upon you when your enemies…will level you to the ground and your children within you…because you did not recognize the time of your visitation" (Luke 19:41-44).

Jesus wept over Jerusalem because they had rejected Him, their Messiah. Sin had deceived them. Jerusalem would be destroyed because the Jews would not repent, believe that Jesus was the Christ, and be saved. What the Jews longed for—the Messiah and His kingdom, heaven, and eternal life—they would miss. And the One who could have saved them and given them all this wept audibly.

The second account of Jesus weeping is at the tomb of Lazarus.

The third time Jesus weeps is when He faces the awful hell of death when He will be separated from the Father. In Hebrews 5, we get a glimpse not given in other accounts of the agony of our Lord in the Garden of Gethsemane: "In the days of His flesh, He offered up both prayers and supplications with loud crying and tears to the One able to save Him from death, and He was heard because of His piety" (5:7).

Jesus wept in the face of death's separation, for He was to be made sin for us and, in becoming sin, He would "taste death for everyone" (Hebrews 2:9; 2 Corinthians 5:21). For the first time in all of eternity, Jesus would be separated from the Father. The Life and Light of the world would wage war against death and darkness, and He would win!

Death was not an unconquerable enemy. It was not an impossible, impassable barrier for the Son of Man and of God who came to take away sin. Death will have to release its captives at the sound of His voice even as when He cried, "Lazarus, come forth" (John 11:43). "For an hour is coming, in which all who are in the tombs will hear His voice, and will come forth…" (John 5:28,29).

# 114

Can you imagine watching Jesus Christ command a dead man to come forth from the grave and then seeing him appear upon command, and still refusing to believe that Jesus was sent from God? When Jesus said, "Lazarus, come forth," Lazarus was actually propelled to the door of the tomb. It was as if a giant magnet of life pulled him out of death's magnetic field!

Lazarus had been "bound hand and foot with wrappings, and his face was wrapped around with a cloth" (John 11:44). He could neither move nor see in the darkness of that tomb how to get out of it. His eyes were covered with grave clothes, as were his arms and legs. Until someone loosed him and let him go, he could not move. There was no way even a live man bound in grave clothes could have come forth from the tomb.

Jews believed that the soul of a dead person hovered about the body until the third day, when corruption began and the soul took flight. I believe Jesus purposely waited until four days had passed before He came to raise Lazarus from the dead. I think He wanted to prove conclusively that He was the Resurrection and the Life. Here was the miracle of miracles, the sign of signs that would show Him to be the Christ, the Son of God. Only one sign would remain, and that would be His own resurrection from the dead.

And yet many seeing Lazarus' resurrection still would not believe. In John 11:45,46, we read: "Therefore many of the Jews who came to Mary, and saw what He had done, believed in Him. But some of them went to the Pharisees and told them the things which Jesus had done."

This brings us to our final truth: *Death exposes unbelief.* When a person comes face-to-face with the certainty of imminent death, then he knows whether he has believed or not.

Oh, how I have longed to share more at funerals! I believe that every funeral ought to be a time of confronting family and friends with the gospel of Jesus Christ. Is this not what our Lord did at Lazarus' wake? Of course, for it was then that He asked Martha if she really believed that He was the Christ, God incarnate, the Resurrection and the Life.

Have you told your family what you want done at your funeral? Have you ever thought of how, indirectly, you might have one last opportunity, even in your death, to share the glorious gospel of Jesus Christ?

Death, Beloved, exposes unbelief. Make your death count. Let it expose any unbelief in those attending your funeral. Don't miss the opportunity for life to spring out of your death. Write it in your will: "If no gospel is preached, then no inheritance will be given!"

# Notes

1. From time to time we will look at the definition of a word in the Greek. Since the New Testament was originally written in Koine Greek, sometimes it is helpful to go back to the Greek to see the original meaning of the word. There are many study tools to help you if you would like to do this type of digging. One excellent book that will help you understand how to do more in-depth study is *How to Study Your Bible* (Harvest House).

2. The word translated "again" is *anothen,* and can also be translated "from above."

3. Present tense in the Greek, thereby denoting habitual or continuous action. This does not preclude singular acts of sin.

4. Merrill Tenney, *John: The Gospel of Belief* (Grand Rapids, MI: William B. Eerdmans Publishing Company, 1948), 40-41.

5. Ibid., 103.

6. Marvin R. Vincent, D.D., *Vincent's Word Studies of the New Testament,* vol. 2 (McLean, VA: MacDonald Publishing Company), 158.

7. Lawrence O. Richards, *Expository Dictionary of Bible Words* (Grand Rapids, MI: Zondervan Publishing House, 1985), 313.

8. Ibid., 416.

9. From time to time we will look at the definition of a word in the Hebrew. Since the Old Testament was originally written in Hebrew, sometimes it is helpful to go back to the Hebrew to see the original meaning of the word. There are many study tools to help you if you would like to do this type of digging. One book that will help you understand how to do in-depth study is *How to Study Your Bible* (Harvest House).

10. Herbert Lockyer, D.D., *All the Divine Names and Titles in the Bible* (Grand Rapids, MI: Zondervan Publishing House, 1975), 17.

11. See the New American Standard Bible footnote on this verse.

12. John MacArthur, Jr., *The Legacy of Jesus* (Chicago: Moody Press, 1986), 57.

13. Ibid.

14. W.E. Vine, Merrill F. Unger, William White, Jr., *Vine's Complete Expository Dictionary of Old and New Testament Words* (Nashville: Thomas Nelson Publishers, 1985), 251.

15. Richards, *An Expository Dictionary of Bible Words,* 119.

16. Archibald Thomas Robertson, *Word Pictures in the New Testament,* vol. 5 (Nashville: Broadman Press, 1932, renewal 1960), 202.

# HARVEST HOUSE BOOKS
## BY KAY ARTHUR

*God, Are You There?*
*His Imprint, My Expression*
*How to Study Your Bible*
*Israel, My Beloved*
*Just a Moment with You, God*
*Lord, Teach Me to Pray in 28 Days*
*A Marriage Without Regrets*
*A Marriage Without Regrets Study Guide*
*With an Everlasting Love*

## Bibles

*The New Inductive Study Bible* (NASB)